The Unknown Fostering

A study of private fostering

Bob Holman

Russell House Publishing

First published in 2002 by:
Russell House Publishing Ltd.
4 St George's House
Uplyme Road
Lyme Regis
Dorset DT7 3LS

Tel: 01297-443948
Fax: 01297-442722
e-mail: help@russellhouse.co.uk

British Library Cataloguing-in-publication Data:
A catalogue record for this book is available from the British Library.

ISBN: 1-903855-03-9

Typeset by TW Typesetting, Plymouth, Devon

Printed by Bell & Bain, Glasgow

About Russell House Publishing
RHP is a group of social work, probation, education and youth and community work practitioners and academics working in collaboration with a professional publishing team.
Our aim is to work closely with the field to produce innovative and valuable materials to help managers, trainers, practitioners and students. We are keen to receive feedback on publications and new ideas for future projects.

Contents

Part Three

Private Fostering Today and Tomorrow

Foreword

As a young child care officer in 1962, I was given a number of private foster children on my large caseload in a local authority Children's Department. My interest and concern was aroused and, after I entered academic life, I undertook a Ph.d about private fostering. The results were published in 1973. (Holman, 1973) After that time my studies and practice concentrated on issues like poverty and activities like neighbourhood work but I always retained an interest in private fostering. Once I entered my sixties, I wanted again to focus on private fostering in what would probably be my last piece of research. This time I wanted less of a statistical investigation and more one that was rooted in the experiences and perceptions of former private foster children, private foster carers and welfare professionals who specialised in private fostering.

My thanks are due, as so often, to Eric Adams and the Barrow Cadbury Trust which made a grant for the study. Brendan McGrath, a social worker with extensive experience and knowledge about private fostering, was not only one of the interviewees but also kindly read and amended the final chapter. Kriss Akabusi and David Donnison – both of them former private foster children – have also been very helpful. Geoffrey Mann of Russell House Publishing was a source of encouragement. I am blessed with a loving and supportive family with my wife Annette, our son David, our daughter Ruth, son-in-law Bruce, and lovely grandson Lucas. I thank them for the happiness they give me.

After I sent this book to the publishers in October, 2001, some attention has been drawn to private fostering by the British Agencies for Adoption and Fostering (BAAF). It commissioned Terry Philpot to compile a report on private fostering called *A Very Private Practice. An Investigation into Private Fostering*. After an admirable short summary of the state of private fostering, Philpot is scathing about the lack of local authority interest in private foster children for whom they have some statutory obligations to protect. Amongst the Social Services Departments he contacted, one confused it with those independent (sometimes called 'private' agencies) which have contracts with the departments to find foster homes for children who are in the care of local authorities. Another, which offered no private fostering service at all, said that it was being undertaken on their behalf by a voluntary project. Yet it had not consulted the project! In another authority, Philpot records, 'One person, said to have responsibility (for private fostering), laughed when I asked if, in fact, that was the case and said: "Well, yes – theoretically but I don't know much about it." ' (Philpot, 2001, p33). Others said that the low numbers of private foster children did not justify a service or that private fostering was not one of their priorities.

Philpot also criticises the complacency of central government. The Department of Health has failed to mount an effective campaign to inform the public about private fostering. Further, government, to date, has refused to legislate for the registration of private foster carers by local authorities so that it would be an offence to take private foster children without being on the approved register. Philpot notes that the government's explanation for this refusal is that 'the primary responsibility for safeguarding the welfare of the privately fostered child rests with the parent' (p39). Philpot then sharply points out that this ignores the obvious fact that even the best intentioned parents cannot gain access to police records, or know whether their child's carer has had her own children removed by the local authority.

Philpot concluded that 'there is irrefutable evidence that privately fostered children are, mostly, a group at risk, they are also a group who lack protection through a combination of inaction by both central and local government' (p5). His recommendations include that registration should become law, that each local authority should appoint a designated social work manager with responsibility for private fostering and that the local authority should have a duty to offer support to young people who were in private foster homes three months before their 16th birthday.

BAAF launched the Philpot report at a well-attended press conference in November, 2001, although subsequent coverage was over-shadowed by events in Afghanistan. It coincided with the appearance in the House of Commons of the Adoption and Children Bill. Hilton Dawson MP then put forward an amendment to the bill to allow for the registration of private foster carers.

Hopefully the government will accept the amendment so that, in the not too distant future, local authorities will have to compile a register. However, this legislation will not be sufficient. Registration will only be effective if the public, natural parents, carers and welfare professionals are aware of the obligation to register. Further, local authorities will only be able to seek out private fosterings, assess the private foster carers, support those who are approved, protect the children and maintain contact with the natural parents if they have sufficient resources for these tasks. I attempt to address this issue in the last chapter of this book.

But central and local government will only act if they are under pressure so to do. The most powerful – and probably the unqiue part of this volume – is part two which contains interviews with adults who were private foster children, with private foster carers and with welfare professionals who do specialise in private fostering. Bored readers can skim over my ramblings but should read what these private fostering participants have to say. Their words powerfully demonstrate the dangers, the benefits and the potential of private fostering. Their experiences should convince government that action is necessary now.

Bob Holman

Part One
Private Fostering 1850–2000

Chapter 1: The Baby Farmers 1850–1948

Private fostering is essentially about children placed by their parents or guardians to live with non-relatives in the latter's own homes. It is to be distinguished from children placed by public agencies with foster parents chosen and supervised by the agencies.

Private fostering, no doubt, is as old as history. Mary Hopkirk has documented a number of historical cases of parents, particularly unmarried mothers, farming out, giving away, and even selling their children to strangers who subsequently neglected them (Hopkirk, 1949).

Victorian Times

Private fostering appeared to multiply during the Victorian era following rapid industrialisation and urbanisation. The number of illegitimate births increased with unmarried mothers often left with the choice of entering the workhouse with their baby or finding a job and someone else to care for their child. It was not just single mothers. In some areas, particularly in mill towns in Lancashire, married mothers went out to work and had to find other women prepared to look after their young children. The standard of care provided by the foster mothers often led much to be desired and the founding of the Infant Life Protection Society in 1870 marked a growing concern with the treatment of babies and a questioning of the fact that private foster parents were subject to no official inspections. The mortality rate amongst infants under one year old farmed-out in large cities was estimated at between 70–90 per cent. During the same period, a number of inquests and prosecutions made it clear that some private foster mothers were murdering the children for financial gain. The children, their lives having been insured with several burial clubs, would be murdered by an excessive use of opiates, commonly used to keep babies quiet, by burning, scalding, by suffocating or by neglect. The case of the notorious foster mother, Mrs Margaret Waters, who was executed in 1870 for the murder

1

and manslaughter of five children, was one of the factors leading to the establishment of the Select Committee on the Protection of Infant Life. Its report, published in 1871, uncovered a widespread system of what was called 'baby-farming.' In many cases, the children of the mostly unmarried mothers were taken by the foster mothers for adoption, where frequently they died, while in others the mothers maintained contact because they made payments.

The report led to the first Infant Life Protection Act (1872). Under its provisions, private foster mothers who took in two or more children aged under one for reward, that is for material gain, were required to register with the local authority to prove their fitness for the work. The local authority could refuse to register any house which it considered unsuitable and strike off the register any person incapable of providing proper food and attention or guilty of serious neglect. The death of any foster child had to be reported to a coroner. It was made clear that persons fostering relatives or taking children from public institutions, such as the Poor Law, were exempted from these provisions.

The Act, for all its fine intentions, was never fully implemented, not least because it failed to lay the duties and powers upon any specific local authority committee or department. The horror stories continued with attention focussed not just on London and northern manufacturing towns but also on Glasgow and Edinburgh. The Scottish National Society for the Prevention of Cruelty to Children publicised a number of cases about infant private foster children such as the following in 1890:

> *They were put in little chairs in corners of the room, where they had bottleless teats put in their mouths . . . the nursed children were seldom fed at all . . . In the day two were always in their wooden chairs. Their thighs became raw by their position and the filth they sat in . . . untended, hungry, thirsty, crying, so they lay, day by day, suffering from measles, until one was taken up to be 'laid out' and the other to be removed to kinder care, where it speedily died. Both children were insured, each for £4.* (cited by Abrams, 1998, p218)

In 1896, another scandalous murder trial of a foster mother, Mrs Dyer, took place. It was followed by the Infant Life Protection Act (1897) which raised the children's upper age limit to which legislation applied, from one to five and placed a duty upon local authorities to inquire in their areas whether there were persons fostering for reward. It also gave local authorities greater powers of inspection and of removal of foster children to a place of safety. The 'improper care' of a child was defined as 'Kept in any house or premises which are so unfit or so overcrowded as to endanger its health; or retained or received by any persons who, by reason of negligence, ignorance or other cause, is so unfit to have its care and maintenance as to endanger its health.' It indicated that inspections should be carried out by committee members and officials of the Poor Law rather than the police.

Once more, inspections of private fosterings were never properly implemented. The Poor Law was mainly geared towards dealing with destitute families, not the ways in which children were looked after. It was not just that the law was not applied. It also contained severe loopholes. It did not deal with private foster homes which took just one child yet, as the *Glasgow Herald* made clear in 1910, private fostering was frequently about unmarried mothers who placed their only child with strangers (cited by Abrams, 1998, p15).

Significantly, by the end of the nineteenth century, the prevailing perceptions of private fostering had been formed. The Victorian focus on baby farms and murderous foster mothers meant that private fostering was invariably seen as a problem. Yet simultaneously it was regarded as a problem which did not justify the same attention given to children fostered, or boarded out, by public bodies like Dr Barnardos or the Poor Law. True enough, the supervision provided by these bodies to the children entrusted to them was insufficient. But, as Jean Heywood explains, detailed regulations were laid down and officials of these agencies did accept responsibility (Heywood, 1959, p118–9). Not so for private foster children. Henceforth, private foster parents were usually seen in a negative light with little focus on the positive contribution they might make. And henceforth, private foster children continued to receive an inferior service from the authorities.

Into the Twentieth Century

Social policy did pay more attention to children in Britain during the twentieth century to the extent that it was sometimes called 'the century of the child.' But private foster children were mainly outside this concern. The Children Act (1908) mainly dealt with child offenders but it did raise the upper age limit of private foster children to seven, made the legislation applicable to foster homes which took one child and clarified that the responsibility for inspecting private fosterings rested with the Poor Law.

The first four decades of the century witnessed the gradual dismantling of the Poor Law with local authority departments taking on more responsibilities. In regard to private fosterings, local health departments began to take over from the Poor Law. Thus it is in the Ministry of Health's *Eighth Annual Report of 1926–27* that it is claimed that the worst abuses of baby-farming had been eradicated. The movement of foster child protection into the health field was confirmed by the Public Health Act (1936), the Public Health (London) Act (1936) and the Young Persons (Scotland) Act (1937) which made provision for what were called 'children maintained for reward'. These were children under nine years of age maintained for reward by persons (other than relatives and legal guardians) who were not their parents. Most statutory and voluntary children's homes and schools were exempted from these provisions but certain institutions and residential nurseries run for profit were included. Under the acts, the carers were obliged to notify the welfare authority before the child was received, not less than seven days for the first child and not less than 48 hours beforehand for any subsequent children. They also had a duty to give at least seven days notice of any change of residence (the time was reduced to 48 hours in the event of an emergency move). They also had to inform the authority and the person from whom the child was received within 48 hours of the death of a foster child or the removal of the child from their care. The welfare authorities, that is the health authorities in England and Wales and the Poor Law in Scotland, were required to appoint child protection visitors to visit and to satisfy themselves as to the health and well-being of the foster children and to give any necessary advice 'from time to time'. The acts also gave the authorities powers to fix the maximum number of children aged under nine who could be kept in any particular premises. If a foster child was about to be received into or was already in overcrowded, insanitary or dangerous premises, or by any persons unfit to have the care of children or in any environment detrimental to the child, the welfare authority could apply to a court for an order to remove them to a place of safety. The inspection was usually entrusted to health visitors while the service was under the general supervision of the Ministry of Health.

It is worth adding that, following the Adoption of Children (Regulation) Act (1939) and the Adoption Society Regulations of 1943, children aged under nine placed for adoption by persons who were not their parents, often called 'third party placements', also became subject to the provisions of the above Public Health Acts until an adoption order was made. As this book is particularly concerned with private fostering rather than adoption, no further consideration will be given to these children in this volume.

In his study of the treatment of children in the care of the community in the first half of the twentieth century, *When Family Failed*, Nigel Middleton regrets that information about children maintained for reward 'is non-existent' (Middleton, 1971, p225). The days of large-scale baby-farming appeared to be over and it was considered that most private foster children were illegitimate children placed by unmarried mothers. But the matter was not discussed in parliament, did not catch the interest of the press, was not studied by academics and was not a concern of the emerging social work occupations. At least some figures became available. By the end of 1944, there were 10,693 children in private foster homes in England and Wales and, in May 1945, the number in Scotland was 1,363. The following years were to see significant changes in the child care legislation of Britain.

Chapter 2: The Children's Departments and Private Fostering 1948–1970

The Second World War unexpectedly proved a turning point in the development of services for deprived children. The mass evacuation of children, of whom I was one, focussed greater attention on the needs of children separated from their own parents. Lady Marjory Allen led a campaign to persuade the government to mount an inquiry into the methods of care for children 'deprived of a normal home life'. The wartime debate about child care was mainly about children looked after by public authorities but the needs of private foster children were noted by officials in two directions. During the war, the percentage of illegitimate births in the United Kingdom increased from 4.4 to 9.1 per cent. As private fostering was mainly concerned with the placement of illegitimate children, it was expected that the number with private foster parents would increase. Further, the Ministry of Health expressed concerns that, by the end of the war, many evacuees would be abandoned by their parents while others would be orphans. If they stayed with their wartime foster parents, would they constitute private foster homes?

The campaign prompted the government to set up two committees of inquiry whose reports were published in 1946. The Curtis Report, *Report of the Care of Children Committee*, applied to England and Wales and the Clyde Report, *Report of the Committee on Homeless Children*, to Scotland.

The two reports were mainly concerned with the standards of and organisation of services for children looked after by public agencies. They recommended that local authorities should establish Children's Departments, overseen by a committee of elected members, the Children's Committee, with no other responsibility than that of looking after deprived children. However, the reports did not ignore private fostering. The Curtis Report indicated that a number of witnesses had expressed concern about private foster children or Child Life Protection cases as they were known officially. It recommended that the Children's Departments take over their responsibility. It then made some specific recommendations:

- It argued that the age limit of nine years be raised to 16 'so that the child may be under supervision until they have left school' (Home Office, Ministry of Health and Ministry of Education, 1946, para. 424).

- It reasoned that private foster children come under supervision whether there was reward or not, that is whether the foster parents were paid or not.

The committee also considered whether private fostering should be brought under the full control of the new department so as 'requiring the mother to consult the children's officer before placement and to place the child only with a foster mother on the approved list.' It concluded with regret 'that to require preliminary notification by the parent as well (as by the foster parent) might lead to widespread evasion and increase in the number of placements without any notification at all' (para. 475). The committee also warmly commended a scheme in Birmingham whereby the local authority guaranteed payments to approved private foster parents for children under five and recovered them from the natural parents. It argued that this would stop some fostering breakdowns caused by lack of payments. It wanted it applied to all private foster children not just those under five.

The Clyde Report in Scotland gave private fostering less attention than Curtis but it agreed that the new department should take over responsibility. It considered that most private placements were made by unmarried mothers for their illegitimate children and acknowledged that the standard of private foster homes 'is generally lower than that selected by the Local Authorities' (Scottish Home Department, 1946, para. 27). The committee believed that relationships between the foster mothers and local authorities would be smoothed if the new department 'guaranteed the payment to the foster mother and collected it from the parent' (para. 106). It also recommended that inspection by the local authority should continue until the child was 18.

The ensuing Children Act (1948), which went through with support from all political parties, accepted the main thrust of the recommendations of the Curtis and Clyde Reports. Children's Departments were established and took over the care of children who had previously been scattered amongst a range of statutory bodies like Education and Public Assistance Departments. The act was widely welcomed as heralding a new era of humane care for deprived children. In regard to private fostering, Part V of the act was devoted to Child Life Protection. The new departments took over the responsibilities as set down in the acts of 1936–37 while the age level of private foster children was extended to the age at which children left school with their supervision continuing until the age of 18 if they remained with the same foster parents.

Noticeably, the Children Act did not take up the recommendations to include as private foster children those for whom no reward was made and it did not place a duty upon local authorities to guarantee payments to private foster parents. Indeed, the duties and powers of the Children's Departments towards private foster homes and the duties in regard to private foster parents to give advance notification to local authorities about taking a child remained much the same as under the 1936–37 legislation.

The Child Life Protection provisions appeared to apply to certain independent residential schools and the effect of extending the age of private foster children from nine to school leaving age meant that many more were drawn into the provisions. There ensued some conflict between a number of Children's Departments which attempted to inspect prestigious private schools who resented their intrusion. Eventually, the schools were exempted.

The Children Act (1958)

In the years following the Children Act (1948), the new Children's Departments were almost overwhelmed with applications for children to be taken into care, with finding more foster homes and raising the standards of residential care. Yet they did not overlook private foster children. The Association of Children's Officers and the Association of Child Care Officers (hereafter referred to as ACO and ACCO) took an interest and lobbied for improved legislation. As I have shown elsewhere, Ian Brown, the children's officer for Manchester, one of the busiest authorities in Britain, did not ignore the needs of private foster children (Holman, 1996). He was particularly upset by a case in 1956. A health visitor came across a four month old baby with a private foster mother who had not given notification but when a child care officer called, the family had moved: the health visitor found them again but the foster mother passed the baby on to another woman without informing the Children's Department and soon after, the baby died from acute bronchitis. Brown became an advocate for better legislation. The Home Office inspectors responsible for child care also took an interest in private fostering and always gave some space to them in their periodic reports. There followed the Children Act (1958) which drew together and made additions to the legislation about private fostering. The main sections of the new act were as follows:

Section 1 placed a duty on local authorities to visit private foster children 'from time to time' and 'to satisfy themselves as to the well-being of the children and give such advice as to their care and maintenance as may appear to be needed.'

Section 2 defined a private foster child as one, 'below the upper limit of compulsory school age whose care and maintenance are undertaken for reward for a period exceeding one month by a person who is not a relative or guardian.'

Section 3 placed a duty on private foster parents to give notice of their intention to take a child at least two weeks before the child was received. In the case of an emergency, the notice should be made not later than one week after the child arrived. When the child was moved to another foster home, the foster parents were obliged to inform the local authority within 48 hours.

Section 4 empowered local authorities to prohibit placements where they were 'of the opinion that it would be detrimental to that child to be kept by them (foster parent) in those premises.'

Section 6 of this act specified certain persons as being so unsuitable that they were open to the designation 'disqualified person' in regard to taking private foster children and could not do so unless the local authority gave its consent. These were persons who had had a child removed from them as being in 'need of care and protection' under the Children and Young Persons Act (1933), who had had their rights over a child removed by a resolution passed under Section 2 of the Children Act (1948), who had been convicted of any offences specified in the First Schedule of the Children and Young Persons Act (1933) which particularly dealt with sexual offences, who had been refused registration or had had such registration cancelled by the health authority to be a child minder.

Section 7 allowed local authorities to complain to a juvenile court that a child was being kept by a 'person unfit to have their care' or in premises detrimental to them. The case being proved, the court could make an order to remove the child to a place of safety. In cases of imminent danger, the order could be made by a Justice of the Peace. Children so removed could be received into the care of the local authority. Appeals by the foster parents could be taken to a higher court.

The Leicestershire Children's Department

An example of the work of a Children's Department with private fostering can be found in the annual reports of the Leicestershire children's officer, Miss K. L. Ruddock. In the first report for 1948–49, she noted that the Children's Department had taken over responsibility for 61 children from the Health Department. She observed that, 'In general the homes are satisfactory but a few give cause for anxiety' (Ruddock, 1949, p11). In 1950–51, she pointed out that natural parents were often erratic in making payments to the private foster parents. Miss Ruddock regretted that the department's powers to help and intervene were limited. However, she added, 'In certain cases it has been possible to receive the children into care under Section 1 of the Children Act and approve the foster home as an official one' (Ruddock, 1951, p10). Action of this kind was rare for it depended on the natural parents agreeing to the children being received into care and upon the foster parents being of the same standard as local authority ones.

By 1961, the number of private foster children in Leicestershire had dropped to 23. Then it began to climb again. In the report of 1961–63, Miss Ruddock wrote, 'The most interesting aspect of this rise is the number of coloured children placed by their own parents. These are not unwanted half-caste children, but fully coloured and much wanted children, with both parents in this country. The father is almost always taking a training course of some kind, and the mother may also be training, or may have taken a job to help the family finances . . . the child care officers are getting quite adept at pronouncing names like Olowake Njandolo. The foster mothers normally give their charges easier nicknames like

Bunty or Sambo, and grow very attached to these attractive piccaninnies' (Ruddock, 1963, pp8–9).

In 1967–69, the children's officer recorded that the number of private foster children was 87, with the 'coloured' ones being mainly West African. She was now very concerned about their care and wrote, 'There is a tendency for some foster mothers to take in too many children, with the resultant danger of poor care and 'baby farming' attitudes. It has not been necessary to take court action but on two occasions parents have been asked to make other plans ... on the other hand, some African parents move their children around far too often, and some of these small children show signs of insecurity and deprivation which cause concern' (Ruddock, 1969, p10).

West African Foster Children

Packman pointed out, 'The 11,000 children in private foster homes recorded by Curtis in 1946, had shrunk to 7,411 by 1949, which might mean that a substantial number of placements were terminated after the war or were made official by taking the children into care under the Children Act' (Packman, 1975, p77). After 1960, however, the numbers as issued by the Home Office for England and Wales, rose again. In 1961 it was 6,780, in 1963 it climbed to 8,038 and in 1969 it reached 10,907. The increase was almost certainly due to West African foster children.

Advertisements from African students seeking foster parents for their children began to appear in *Nursery World* in 1955. The Leicestershire and other children's officers started to record their presence in the early 1960s. The Home Office report for 1964–66 not only noted the record level of private foster children at 10,600 but also pointed out that the increase was mainly in London and Kent 'due in large part to the number of overseas students seeking foster homes for their children' (Home Office, 1967). Beyond doubt, more West African students were coming to study in Britain and their use of foster homes explained the increase. The difficulties they experienced was such that in 1961, Mr B.B. Boateng founded the Commonwealth Students' Children Society to help West African students and their families.

Increased Interest

The rise in numbers, coupled with the new legislation of 1958, provoked the interest of the child care occupations. ACO monitored the situation and Ian Brown backed its recommendation that legislation was required to:

- Make natural parents, as well as foster parents, responsible for informing the local authority about an intended placement.
- Place on local authorities a duty to visit private foster children the same number of times as local authority foster children.

- Give local authorities the power to maintain a register in which foster parents would have to be accepted before they could take children.

(Holman, 1996, p95)

ACCO also kept the subject before its committees, lobbied MPs about possible changes in the law, and often had comments in its journal *Child Care News*. Its legal sub-committee agreed with the proposals of ACO and also wanted the term 'emergency', under which foster parents could delay giving notification, more closely defined.

Occasional reports which reflected badly on private fostering began to appear in the press. For instance, in 1965 a fostering couple were jailed for neglecting and ill-treating a five year old Nigerian boy. These cases were not akin to the banner headlines in today's press about child abuse. They rarely covered more than a few paragraphs and they were not used as a stick for beating social workers. But they did add to the warnings being voiced by the professional associations.

A small number of MPs then took up the issue of private fostering. Most prominent was the Labour member Leo Abse who, in 1968, led an all-party delegation to the Home Secretary. The delegation expressed its dismay that, as most private fosterings were not notified in advance to the Children's Departments, children could be handed to private foster parents without any checks, with the contact perhaps made by a postcard in a stationer's shop. It also voiced concern over a number of 'tug-of-love' cases in which natural parents had had difficulties in reclaiming their children. James Callaghan, the Home Secretary promised to look into the matters with a view to incorporating proposals into forthcoming legislation in 1969. A few months later, his memory must have been jogged when the press reported the death of a five year old Nigerian girl in a private foster home. The coroner recorded death due to natural causes but it emerged that in 1966 a local authority had obtained a court order to remove a foster child from the woman and declared her a disqualified person. None the less, she had continued to foster. Another case to hit the newspapers concerned an unmarried mother who placed her baby in the care of a 66 year old pensioner and signed over a sixpenny stamp in the belief that this made it legal. The mother then disappeared and the case only came to light when the female pensioner fell ill and the child had to be received into care.

By the end of the 1960s, private fostering, particularly West African fostering, was a child care issue. Certainly it was not a major topic of national debate but it was on the agenda of ACO and ACCO while a few MPs had put pressure on the Home Office whose ministers and officials then entered into discussions with representatives of local authorities. The outcome was that private fostering legislation was attached to the Children and Young Persons Act (1969). This major piece of legislation was primarily to do with juvenile offending with only seven of its 73 sections applying to private fostering. The main ones can be summarised as follows:

- The definition of private foster children was extended to include those for whom reward (payment) was not given. The basic definition thus became, 'a child below the upper limit of compulsory school age whose care and maintenance are undertaken by a person who is not a relative or guardian of theirs' (Section 52).
- Notification was changed so as not to mean notification for every child but to the intent of the person to foster in general. It stated that notification was not required in respect of a child if 'the (foster parent) has on a previous occasion given notice under that subsection of that for any other child ...' (Section 53). Similarly, the foster parent did not have to give notification for each child that left but only when she ceased to be a foster parent.
- The powers of local authorities to prohibit placements were strengthened. They could act if they were of the opinion that the premises or the person was not suitable or if 'it would be detrimental to be kept by that person in those premises' (Section 55). The 1958 Act had seemed to apply that prohibition could be applied only to unsuitable premises, now there was no doubt that it also applied to persons.
- The duty placed upon local authorities by the 1958 Act to visit private foster children 'from time to time' in order to satisfy themselves as to the well-being of the children was replaced by a duty to visit from time to time where they think it 'appropriate' (Section 51).

ACO, ACCO and the MPs who had lobbied for change were pleased that the 'reward' element was removed from the definition of private fostering and that the powers of local authorities to prohibit placements had been clarified. But the other provisions baffled them. The new notification provisions meant that notification did not have to be given for every individual child. Home Office officials explained that it would reduce paperwork but ACCO pointed out that it would now be legal for some children to come and go without the authorities having to be informed. These criticisms were taken on board and subsequent legislation made it clear that every child had to be accounted for. The officials defended the insertion of the word 'appropriate' after the duty to visit 'from time to time' on the grounds that it made it 'more flexible'. By contrast the child care bodies had considered the duty already too flexible and had wanted the number of visits to be specified. ACCO and ACO were also disappointed that the Act did not implement their suggestions to place a duty upon natural parents (as well as foster parents) to give notification when a child was placed, to define 'emergency' more tightly, and to empower local authorities to keep a register of approved private foster parents.

It is to the credit of many Children's Departments that, despite the enormous pressures on them, they did give some attention to private fosterings. Even more so, ACO and ACCO frequently raised their concerns about the conditions of the children and pressed for more effective legislation: with some, but limited success. However, the latter half of the 1960s was overshadowed by the much larger issue of the wholesale reform of the personal social services which was to see the abolition of Children's Departments.

Chapter 3: Social Services Departments and Private Fostering 1970–1980

The Social Work (Scotland) Act of 1968 completely reorganised local authority personal social services in Scotland. It amalgamated certain local authority departments, including the Children's Departments into larger Social Work Departments (SWDs). The reform went beyond that which eventually happened south of the border in that the Act also established Children's Hearings in which lay panels, not courts, dealt with young offenders and non-offenders. Only one of the 99 sections of the Act dealt with private fostering. It stated that the Children Act (1958) would still be applicable in Scotland.

In England and Wales, the Local Authority Social Services Act (1970) also amalgamated a number of departments and parts of others into Social Services Departments (SSDs). The duties of Children's Departments towards private fostering were transferred to these SSDs.

Trends in Child Care

The establishment of new services and the pouring in of public money seemed to miss out private fostering. Many of the SSDs and the SWDs went 'generic', that is their social workers were given mixed caseloads of deprived children, elderly people, those with mental health problems and so on. Former child care officers struggled to understand the provisions for disabled people while former welfare officers had to come to grips with child care law. Social workers burdened with these demands and coping with a much larger bureaucracy appeared to have little time for private foster children. Within a few years, departments began to switch back to more specialist approaches but by this time much child care expertise had been lost. The Association of Directors of Social Services (ADSS) and the British Association of Social Workers (BASW) displayed less interest in and lobbied less for private foster children than had the now defunct ACO and ACCO. None the less, trends in child care were emerging which did have implications for private fostering.

In 1973, Maria Colwell, a child in the care of the local authority which had returned her to her mother and step-father, suffered a horrific death at their hands. Child abuse became national headlines and there followed, in the next three decades, some 40 public inquiries into the fate of physically and sexually abused children. Social workers were frequently blamed for what happened to the children. SSDs and SWDs then made child abuse the major focus of statutory child care work. Resources were poured into monitoring abused or 'at risk' children while less effort went into preventing children having to enter public care. Private foster children lost out in two directions. The abuse of private foster children never became a major concern of the new departments as they concentrated on children for whom they had more direct responsibility. Further, the hope that prevention might embrace work with the private fostering participants to enable the natural parents to retain care of their children and to improve the care given by foster parents to private foster children never materialised.

1973 also saw the publication of a British edition of an influential American book, *Beyond the Best Interests of the Child* (Goldstein, Freud and Solnit, 1973). It drew upon psychoanalytic theory to assert that children could not relate satisfactorily to two sets of parent figures, that is with their natural and substitute parents. The authors argued that children, who were removed from their natural parents and not returned quickly to them, should be legally and permanently left with their carers. This doctrine coincided with media focus on abusing parents and there emerged what was called the permanency movement. It found expression in the Children Act (1975) which, amongst many other provisions, made it easier for foster parents to adopt their foster children and introduced custodianship orders under which, in certain circumstances, substitute parents gained legal custody of the children (in fact, custodianship orders did not come into effect for a decade). These powers had been intended mainly to help local authority foster parents but they could also be used by private foster parents. In addition, the Act gave the Secretary of State powers to make regulations about the number of times officials should visit private foster children and to require natural parents to give notice when they put children in private foster homes. However, such regulatory powers were not taken up for some years.

Race and Private Fostering

Private fostering was rarely in the news in the early 1970s but the matter of permanency did arise in the courts. Substitute carers in Britain have long had the right to apply to the high court for children to be made wards of court (while remaining with them instead of their natural parents). From the late 1960s, some private foster parents used this process in an attempt to stop children being taken home. The new element was the racial one, it was white carers using the courts to retain black children. West African students were at a disadvantage in wardship proceedings as they often lacked the means or the know-how to obtain expert legal representation. Some parents, who had actually gone back to West Africa in the expectation that friends could arrange for their children to be accompanied home, sometimes found that the private foster parents refused to comply and then found themselves not only without access to British solicitors but also unable to appear in court themselves. Even when the natural parents were represented and could appear in court, the decisions often went against them.

In December 1972, the President of the High Court Family Division decided that a Ghanian girl should stay with her foster parents. The parents were a student and his wife who had placed their daughter at the age of three months and visited about six times a year. When the girl was nine, the parents wanted to return to Ghana with her. The private foster parents, who had no children of their own, refused to part with the girl and had her made a ward of court.

The President, Sir George Baker, stated that his decision was for the best interests of the child. He explained that the girl wanted to stay with her foster parents. He added that the case raised problems of race, nationality, colour and language of a girl who had spent all her formative years in an English suburban culture. He continued 'I think the public, particularly potential foster parents, ought to know of the practice and customs of West African and other coloured people who come to this country, often with the husband a student and the wife working, and a child, perhaps born here, fostered out privately ... The West African sees no harm in this, because under their native law children are brought up by other members of the tribe but the parents retain all their rights. There is here revealed a most disquieting situation, a grave social problem, it has been called a social evil, by which children's lives are ruined' (*The Guardian*, 1972).

The natural parents were devastated by the judge's decision. The father declared that he could not go to Ghana without his daughter as his family would think that he had sold her. Not surprisingly, the case provoked much public interest. One legal commentator acknowledged that the paramount interest had to be 'the welfare of the child' and that, in the short term, her happiness was secured by remaining with the foster parents. However, he raised doubts as to whether her long term interests were served by cutting her links with her Ghanian culture. He continued, 'The African parents had never intended to forfeit their parental rights' and that in West Africa fostering was practised without any question of losing them. He concluded 'In effect, therefore, an immigrant practice has been disapproved' (Diogenes, 1973).

It is not possible to enumerate how many 'tug-of-love' cases involved West African private foster children but certainly there were others. Soon after the above ruling, a similar one was made about a five year old Nigerian girl. She had been born in England and, at four months of age, her parents placed her with private foster parents who had responded to their advertisement. The natural parents later separated and divorced. When the mother wanted to take her daughter back to Nigeria, the foster parents refused to hand her back and had her made a ward of court. The case eventually went to appeal and in 1973 the court ordered that the girl should continue to be a ward of court in the care of the foster parents with the natural mother allowed access.

These and other similar judgements may have been a partial reflection of the success of the permanency movement in defining 'the welfare of the child' to mean primarily staying long term with substitute parents. West African parents may also have had the odds stacked against them for other reasons. Mention has already been made of their difficulties in obtaining high standard legal representation. In addition, their low incomes and poor housing conditions, which compared badly with those of the foster parents, may also have been factors which influenced judges when considering the future of the children.

If nothing else, these cases did draw attention to the fact that numbers of private foster children were West African and that their backgrounds, experiences and futures were different from white private foster children. Worryingly, the statements by the judges implied that British culture and child rearing methods were superior to those of West Africa. Moreover, they appeared to give insufficient attention to the implications of black children remaining with white foster parents. Interestingly, following the case of the five year old Nigerian girl, a welfare officer from the Nigerian High Commission stated, 'This judgment will be a lesson to all African people in England on the question of fostering. Black people who seek English foster parents should be warned of the danger of losing their children' (report in *The Guardian*, 16 February, 1973). The danger was real. It might have been lessened if local authority social workers had spoken on their behalf, perhaps emphasising the parenting abilities of the natural parents and their commitment towards their children, perhaps explaining to the courts the long term implications for black children left with white carers. But in none of the reported cases do they appear to have played any part.

Research on Private Fostering

The public and professional discussion, such as it was, about private fostering was based on the cases which came to court, reports from the Commonwealth Students' Children Society, occasional views put forward by social workers, and the annual numbers of private foster children issued by the government. Whereas a number of studies about local authority fosterings were published in the 1960s and 1970s, there was no systematic research into private fostering. It was not known for certain how local authorities discharged their duties towards private foster children, how the children were treated, who were the private foster parents, and, indeed, why natural parents used private foster homes.

In 1973 my research, *Trading in Children: A Study of Private Fostering* appeared (Holman, 1973). The field work was carried out in the days of the Children's Departments although, by the time of publication, these had been absorbed into the SSDs and SWDs. It constituted the first major investigation with its study group made up of all the notified private foster children, 143 in all, in two adjoining departments. For purposes of comparison, the children were matched with 143 local authority foster children. Information about the fosterings was obtained from the files of the Children's Departments, from interviews with child care officers responsible for the children, from interviews with the foster parents, from interviews with a limited number of natural parents and from questionnaires sent to schools.

The private fosterings were categorised as of three main kinds. The largest group (54.2%) were placed by West African students. The parents were regarded as students although not all were full-time students. Deserted spouses (17%) made up the next group who placed their children in private foster homes so that they could go out to work. The third group, unmarried mothers (15.3%), also wanted to work and so put their illegitimate children in private foster homes. The remaining 13 per cent were scattered amongst a variety of parents. The study thus confirmed what child care officers had been saying, namely that West African children made up a substantial part of private fosterings.

Those natural parents who were interviewed were asked why they used private fostering? Why not use day care? In regard to West Africans, a contemporary explanation was that fostering was a part of their culture. Yet from the discussions with the parents, it became clear that fostering was by no means universal practice in West Africa, that the fosterings which did occur were usually with relatives and that those placed were not babies but usually went as older children in order to learn a trade or be closer to schools. Obviously this was very different from private fostering in Britain. Some West African parents said that they had initially sought day care but found that local authority day nurseries did not give priority to students while daily minders proved more expensive than private fostering. Numbers of the students worked shifts and evenings which did not fit in with the hours of day care. Not least, the West Africans were often in crowded rooms and faced difficulties in finding affordable accommodation which would take children. They therefore turned to private fostering, a step which may have been made more acceptable because they were familiar with fostering, howbeit of a different kind, back home.

A few West Africans had approached Children's Departments for help only to be told that their needs did not fit with those for which the local authority could intervene. By contrast, the position of the deserted spouses and unmarried mothers, who were using private foster homes, were very similar to those whose children had been taken into care and were numbered amongst the local authority control group. It emerged that statutory officers made differing decisions about similar applicants. They accepted some children but argued that other unmarried mothers and deserted spouses were capable of looking after them. These parents then turned to private fostering. In addition, other parents did not first approach the Children's Departments because they wanted to make their own arrangements and were opposed to the idea of their children being in public care.

Whatever the reasons for the placements, I was concerned to know more about the people with whom they were placed. The private foster parents tended to be from lower working class backgrounds but were not driven by the notion of making money for a third pointed out that the natural parents did not pay regularly. 56 per cent of the private foster parents were fostering for the first time but others were very experienced with 27 per cent having an average of 11 previous foster children. Typically, the private foster mothers, and it was the women not the husbands who took the initiative, looked after pre-school children.

How suitable were the private foster parents? I attempted to gauge this in two ways:

- By noting from the files, factors which the child care officers considered should count against any one wishing to foster, such as having been convicted of an offence against a child, having treated previous children in inadequate ways, and having had their own children removed into public care. 55 per cent of the private foster parents had such factors recorded against them.
- Asking the child care officers if they would have approved the private foster parents to be local authority foster parents. They would not have approved 55 per cent. In fact, 19 per cent of the private foster parents had applied to the local authorities and been rejected.

Clearly, over half of the private foster parents were of dubious quality. Yet the study also stressed that the child care officers would have approved 45 per cent of the private foster parents. Indeed, 24 per cent had been accepted and were taking both private and local authority children.

The research discovered that over a third of the private foster children met their foster parents via an advertisement. For just under a third, the introduction came through a friend or relative. Once the contact was made, the children were usually moved in without any introductory visits. Indeed, over two thirds of the children never met their private foster mother until they went to live there. The private foster mothers were likely to be given only the barest details about the children's previous experiences and current needs. The children's relationships were then made largely with the private foster mothers: over 15 per cent of the private foster fathers were not in favour of taking foster children and only a minority participated fully in their upbringing.

Given the manner in which the children were placed along with the unsuitability of some of the foster parents, it was not surprising that the research found that the emotional and physical condition of the private foster children compared badly with the local authority children: themselves a deprived group. The private foster children were far more likely to display aggression, anxiety and difficulties in making relationships. They were more prone to bronchitis and other respiratory illnesses. Of those at school, their schoolteachers assessed that 29 per cent needed some form of special education.

Only 29 natural parents of the private foster children were interviewed but the findings offered some useful indicators. Whatever their category, students, separated spouses or unmarried mothers, they tended to receive low incomes, to live in privately rented rooms or flats and to be in touch with few relatives. Interestingly, they were more likely to visit their children regularly than those parents whose children were in local authority foster homes. 64 per cent of the private foster children saw at least one parent at least once a month. On the other hand, 16 per cent of the private foster children saw a parent less than once a year and their foster mothers often assumed that they would keep them for good.

The research showed that contact between the Children's Departments and the private fostering participants was minimal. 94 per cent of the placements did not come to the notice of the Children's Departments until after the children were there so the local authorities could not use their powers to prohibit unsatisfactory intended placements. Yet they did not act even in the minority of cases where they did know. The child care officers explained that they were doubtful if their evidence about the private foster homes would stand up in court and, further, that even if they did ban one fostering the natural parents might use another just as bad. Once the children were in the private foster homes, the child care officers indicated that they disapproved of about a third of them staying there but not one officer was prepared to go to court to effect a removal. They said that their departments' own care facilities were stretched to breaking point so that, even if the court did make an order for the child's removal and committal into public care, they would not know where to put them.

Less than 3 per cent of the private foster homes received an average of ten or more visits per year from the child care officers. 31 per cent were seen between five and nine times, 52 per cent between one and four times, while 15 per cent were not seen at all. The local authority foster children were visited far more frequently and regularly. The private foster mothers, in general, were not hostile towards the child care officers but they saw little point in the visits. Visits from the child care officers to the natural parents were even more rare. 90 per cent had not been seen at all in one year.

My conclusion from the research was that there were two nations in fostering. I wrote as follows:

Local authority foster children were assured of regular supervision; the Children's Department had a duty to try to reunite them with their parents: their foster parents were guaranteed certain financial and material aid; and if the foster home did not attain standards of child care which satisfied the Children's Department it had sufficient powers to end the placement.

The private foster children were not assured of regular supervision; the local authority was not obliged to work towards reunification with their parents; their foster parents were not guaranteed a regular income; and however low the standards of child care the Children's Department was not likely to affect a removal. Throughout this study the private foster children have been shown to be in adverse material, emotional and educational conditions in comparison with the local authority foster children, to receive inferior treatment and to be less likely to have their needs met. Instead of being compensated by extra attention and services from the Children's Departments, the reverse occurred, so reinforcing their position.

(Holman, 1973, p252)

These strong words did not imply a wholesale condemnation of private fostering. Numbers of the private foster parents provided a satisfactory service. In some ways they were an essential social service meeting a need which local authorities could not address. The thrust of the recommendations arising from the study, therefore, was not about banning private fostering but rather reaching a balance so that private foster children were properly protected while simultaneously encouraging the capable private foster parents. My major recommendation was the establishment of a new legal enactment called 'fostering guardianship' which would be held by local authorities over all private foster children in their areas. Fostering guardianship would place on local authorities an overall duty for the well-being of private foster children and give them specific powers (without approaching the courts) to forbid placements with certain foster parents and to remove children from unsuitable ones. These actions would be subject to appeal to the courts by the foster parents. The local authorities would also be enjoined to visit the private foster children on a regular basis, to contact their natural parents and to provide material help to the natural parents and the private foster homes. Lastly, I recommended that natural parents as well as foster parents should have a duty to inform local authorities of intending placements.

The Ibadan Conference (1975)

My research did confirm that West African children made up a substantial number of the private foster children in Britain. The Commonwealth Students' Children Society (CSCS) had been helping numbers of West African families and expressed its concern to the Nigerian and Ghanaian High Commissions in Britain. A major outcome was the holding of a two-week long, international seminar at the University of Ibadan in Nigeria. Organised by the CSCS and the University of Ibadan, it drew 80 participants from Nigeria, Ghana, Sierra Leone and Britain. The British Council made funds available to fund some delegates while Joan Lestor, the Under Secretary of State at the Foreign and Commonwealth Office attended. The findings were later published under the title, *The African Child in Great Britain* (CSCS, 1975).

Much of the conference involved West African participants explaining the nature of family life in their countries. It was pointed out that child rearing methods and family functioning varied between different West African countries, between tribes within them, and between urban and rural areas. None the less, a number of general points were made, namely that West African families often looked after children not born to them, that these placements in no way meant that the parents did not care for their children, and that it was taken for granted that the children would return to them even if they did not visit them regularly.

Turning to the experiences of West Africans in Britain, other speakers pointed out how difficult it was for black students to obtain or afford day care. They considered that, realistically, the West African parents in Britain had no option but to use private fostering and that the policy emphasis had to be put on improving it. It was recommended that all private fostering placements should be made via the local authority, that private foster children be visited by social workers as often as children in public care, and that more West African adults in Britain be encouraged to act as foster parents.

Running through the conference was the subject of custody with attention drawn both to the cases where parents had failed to obtain the return of their children and also to the implications of the new custodianship order in the Children Bill (which soon became the Children Act of 1975). A barrister, Nigel Murray, concluded:

> *It is most important that the parents should not appear to abandon a child. If a dispute as to custody arises, and the parents are able to produce evidence that they visited the child regularly, the court will feel much more inclined to allow the parents to have custody of their own child.* (CSCS, 1975, p30)

Pat Stapleton, social worker for the CSCS, summed up the conference with these words:

> *Those coming from Britain left with far greater appreciation of the practical implications of differing family structures and attitudes to child rearing, and the role of the extended family in providing security to a child as well as the intensity of feeling about the importance of the blood tie. The West Africans, who were particularly worried and distressed by the custody cases and the possible implications of the new Children's Bill, acquired a greater understanding of the climate of opinion in Britain which had led to the proposed changes in legislation, and the motivation behind the judgments of the courts in the custody cases, leading to determination to encourage their compatriots to be more aware of the problems and to look for alternatives rather than assuming fostering to be an automatic solution.* (1975, p3)

The Ibadan conference was important in that it was the first one both to explain the family patterns which shaped the expectations of West Africans in Britain and also to warn them of the possible risk of losing their children to private foster parents. Unfortunately, it gained little publicity in Britain. Only four SSDs sent officials to the conference. None came from Scotland. The Department of Health, BASW, the ADSS and their Scottish counterparts, the Association of Social Work Directors (ASWD) provided not a single representative between them. Knowledge about private fostering was increasing but statutory officials in Britain did not appear ready to learn.

Pressure for Improvements

The overstretched SSDs may not have been able to improve their work with and interest in private fostering in the 1970s. Fortunately, the CSCS with occasional help from other agencies and individuals made itself heard. It not only provided services for some families, not only organised the Ibadan conference, it also lobbied MPs about the statutory neglect of private foster children and voiced concern about the decisions in custody cases and the implications of the Children Bill as it foreshadowed the Children Act (1975). Pat Stapleton, in a letter to the press in 1974, pointed out 'that there were an estimated 5,000 children of African student parents currently at risk in private foster homes.' She wanted the government to incorporate into the forthcoming act legislation to:

- Make it illegal for any children to be placed in private foster homes except via local authorities or approved voluntary agencies.
- Make it illegal for any individuals to advertise for private foster children.
- And for local authorities to have a duty to supervise private foster children in the same way as it did local authority foster children.

Further pressure sprang from responses to the publication of *Trading in Children* in 1973. A considerable number of newspapers gave it coverage with most urging the government to take action. A number of MPs also reacted to the study and questions about private fostering were asked in both the Lords and the Commons. In the latter in November, 1973, the Conservative minister for Social Services, Sir Keith Joseph, responded by saying that he had been 'shocked' by the findings of the research and added, 'I should not like it to be thought in a debate concerned primarily with the welfare of children, that the Government are not concerned about this large number of unprotected children. We are considering this problem in the wider context of services for pre-school children.' Sir Keith, however, could not pursue the matter for, in 1974, the Conservatives were defeated and Labour came into power.

During the 1970s the Community Relations Commission began to turn its attention to the treatment of children from ethnic minorities. In March 1975 it issued a pamphlet called *Fostering Black Children*. Much of its content was about the way in which local authorities cared for black children who were in public care. It also included a section on the private fostering of black children and recommended that ' . . . the standard of care given to privately fostered children should not be below that given by foster-parents vetted and registered by the local authority' (Community Relations Commission, 1975, p26–7).

The interest of the media and MPs tended to be short-lived. In 1974 came a private fostering tragedy which, it might be thought, would have secured their more lasting interest. It happened in 1974 in Perth. In February of that year, following an argument, a Mrs Sarah Summers stabbed her co-habitee Mr George Clark. He was immediately taken to hospital and she into custody. A social worker was called and found the couple's two younger children with neighbours, Mr David and Mrs Jean Duncan where they had taken themselves. The boys were Robert Summers aged seven and Richard Clark aged three (the child of the cohabitation). The Duncans had previously lived in Dundee where they had been convicted of serious neglect of their own two children. Mr Duncan was sentenced to three months imprisonment and Mrs Duncan placed on two years probation on condition that she did not have any children in her care during the period. Their own children were committed to the care of the local authority. In 1969, the Duncans moved to Perth and in 1972 their children were allowed to return to them. In 1973, the supervision of these children was transferred from Dundee to Perth whose social worker considered that their care was just about satisfactory. The social worker who called on the Duncans once Robert and Richard were there gave the Duncans £2 for food.

Mr Clark soon left hospital and went to the SWD where he agreed that the boys should stay with the Duncans as a private arrangement. The SWD knew that the Duncans had a previous criminal conviction for cruelty to their own children but did not intervene with this placement because to do so would have entailed removing the boys from their neighbourhood, from being close to their father, and probably having to go into a children's home. The latter course was made more complicated by the fact that the children's home had no vacancies. By April, Mr Clark, the health visitor and a teacher were concerned about the boys and suspected that they were being beaten. The social worker arranged for the youngest boy, Richard, to be seen by a doctor. Although the doctor had been told that there was suspicion of child cruelty, he did not notice bruises on Richard's face and he did not examine his back and buttocks on which, as the hospital later revealed, there were further bruises. He concluded that there were no signs of cruelty. In May, Richard had fits, was removed to hospital where it was found that he had multiple bruising inflicted by the foster parents. He suffered a cerebral haemorrhage resulting in severe brain damage. In July 1974, the Duncans were tried and convicted of cruelty with Mrs Duncan being jailed for four years and Mr Duncan for two.

A three person Committee of Inquiry was set up by the Secretary of State for Scotland and met in private. It concluded that if the doctor had noticed the bruises, the subsequent sequence of events might have been avoided. The SWD, it pointed out, had known about the Duncans' previous conviction which made them prohibited persons in regard to private fostering. However, it added that the legislation also allowed departments to give such persons consent to foster and, in this case, the social worker had done so. In so doing, the department had not broken the law. However, it concluded that the SWD 'had made errors of judgment' in allowing the children to stay with the Duncans once warning signs appeared that all was not well (Scottish Education Department and Social Work Services Group, 1975, Section 76). The members added that, in such a complex case, a case conference should have been called at an early stage. Lastly, it commented that at a time when social work was moving away from specialisms to more general approaches, it might be that cases like this required staff with a particular expertise in child care. The tragedy and the report certainly showed the dangers of private fostering and served to strengthen the case of those who were arguing that local authorities should have much greater and explicit duties towards private foster children. Yet the case made little public impact. As Lynn Abrams wrote, the inquiry 'aroused little more than a murmur in contrast with the Maria Colwell inquiry in England some months earlier' (Abrams, 1998, p248). Perhaps because it was in Scotland, perhaps because the child did not die, perhaps because he was not actually in the care of the local authority, neither the media nor MPs mounted a campaign around it.

The Foster Children Act (1980)

To be sure, government ministers and officials did not entirely ignore private fostering. Both Labour and Conservative ministers assured those who lobbied for improvements that the matter was under review. In 1979, the Labour government was replaced by a Conservative one under Margaret Thatcher and it continued the consideration being given to the subject and passed, with little publicity and little debate, the Foster Children Act (1980) with its subtitle The Regulation and Control of Private Fostering. It is to be distinguished from the Child Care Act (1980) which dealt mainly with the children in the care of local authorities.

The act was mainly one of consolidation which drew together legislation scattered amongst other acts. Those who had lobbied for change were disappointed. They had wanted:

- Private placements to be illegal unless made through local authorities or approved voluntary bodies.
- Local authorities to draw up lists of registered private foster parents.
- Local authorities to monitor private foster children as closely as local authority ones.
- Local authorities to ensure that private foster parents were paid and then to reclaim it from the natural parents.
- Local authorities to have a clear duty to keep in touch with the natural parents.

None of these recommendations were heeded. Section 4 of the act did place a duty upon the natural parents to also notify local authorities when placements were made but this section was not implemented. Section 3 empowered the Secretary of State to make regulations under which local authorities ensured the 'well-being' of private foster children but these regulations were slow in forthcoming. Section 15 prohibited the placing of advertisements for foster children unless the individuals making the advertisement published their true name and address. However, the lobbyists would have preferred any advertisements to be prohibited.

Four years later, legislation came for Scotland in the Foster Children (Scotland) Act of 1984. It was similar to that of 1980 but it was swiftly followed by regulations in 1985 which came into effect in 1986. Three are noteworthy:

- First the responsibility of parents to notify local authorities of intended placements was implemented.
- Second, the information to be gathered by local authorities, once they knew a child was to be placed, concerning the suitability of the proposed foster parents and their accommodation, was spelt out. It included enquiries about the background of the foster parents, a statement from their doctor confirming that they had no serious medical problems and a statement from the doctor of the child about their health. If the local authority considered that the proposed placement was not appropriate to the child's needs then they had to immediately inform the parents and foster parents.
- Third, once a placement was made, the regulations specified that in the first year the child should be visited at least every three months and thereafter at least twice a year. Welcome as these changes were, they did depend largely on natural parents or potential foster parents actually notifying the local authority and upon the SWDs actually carrying out their obligations.

The decade of the 1970s witnessed enormous changes in the organisation of the personal social services in Britain with the creation of large SSDs and SWDs with huge budgets compared with the departments they replaced. It might have been thought that they would have given much more attention to private fosterings. It is true that legislation did make minor changes but the supervision of private foster children and foster parents, the relationship between social workers and the participants in private fostering, and the degree of help offered to natural parents, did not improve. What progress in knowledge and understanding was made stemmed more from small voluntary bodies which can take credit for drawing some attention to the difficulties of black parents and black children faced with institutions and systems which were not sensitive to their ethnic and cultural needs. Research showed that the former Children's Departments had not visited private fosterings frequently enough yet the SSDs and SWDs seemed even less involved. Two nations still existed in fostering with private fostering still very much the unknown and neglected one.

Chapter 4: The 1980s and the Children Act (1989)

During the 1970s, the number of private fosterings appeared to decline. The trend gathered force in the 1980s. In England, the figures published by the Department of Health for the 31st March of each year revealed the number of notified private children in 1980 to be 5,614 while by 1988 it was 2,873. What accounts for the decline? Perhaps more single mothers kept their children rather than put them in private foster homes. Perhaps fewer West Africans were coming as students. More likely, the decline was more apparent than real because SSDs and SWDs were obtaining fewer notifications. The last chapter mentioned that the new departments faced enormous work pressures while having fewer social workers equipped with specialist child care skills. It is almost certain that they became even less pro-active in seeking out private foster homes.

In 1986–87, I had some correspondence with Avon SSD, which included the large urban complex of Bristol. It contained 57 notified private foster children but one of its senior officials wrote to me, 'My view is that I think the number of reported cases of private fostering in Avon is extremely low.' He added that his department only heard of the fosterings through casual contacts and that he considered that the numbers in the inner city areas was actually higher than before (Avon SSD, 1987). In 1988, the total number of notified private foster children in inner and outer London was 351. Given the enormous population of Greater London, it is hard to accept this as a realistic figure.

Concentrations of Foster Homes

The Department of Health figures showed that the greatest number of known private foster homes in 1988 were in the Southern Region of England with 975 of which 290 were in Hampshire and 261 in Kent. Within these, and other southern and south western SSDs, private foster children were concentrated in a small number of council estates.

In Hampshire, most private foster children were found on the Leigh Park estate, Havant which had 120 children, all thought to be West African and placed by parents who lived in London. An article in 1983 contained interviews with social workers and private foster parents on the estate. The head of the social

27

work team, Derek Wilson, reckoned that less than 10 per cent of the private foster parents would have met the requirements to be local authority foster parents. He added that he wanted social workers to be more involved with private foster homes but that staff cuts prevented this. His colleague, Steven Binns, said, 'All the work done on black children suggests it's better for them to grow up with a good knowledge of their ethnic origins. And yet many people on the estate would be among the more racially prejudiced members of society.' A private foster parent with 19 years experience and currently with four private foster children complained that she was not getting the payments for two of them and said, 'I'm thinking of giving them up but I'm so attached to them'. The article ended by stating that this foster mother 'confirmed that many foster parents did not register with the local authority, passed children around, and sometimes had as many as nine foster children at a time' (Cook, 1983).

Few local authorities gave much attention to private fostering but three can be highlighted. Wiltshire appointed Angus Geddes to work with private fosterings and he later wrote about his work in Swindon during 1986–90. He discovered that the number of West African children placed there was higher than had been thought. In December 1986, 58 such children were known to the SSD, a number which declined to 37 in December 1988. However, these figures for one date in the year failed to reflect those who stayed for very short periods. Thus during the whole of 1988, 125 West African children spent some time in private placements in Swindon.

Geddes established that in 1988, 61 per cent of the private foster children were aged 0–3 years, 17 per cent 3–5 years, and 21 per cent five or over. Most children appeared to go back to their parents at the ages of three or five. He considered that numbers of the private foster parents were clearly unsuitable. One couple, for instance, had six private foster children although the foster father had a conviction for sexual abuse. Geddes was also concerned that, following arguments with the foster parents, some natural parents often removed their children after one or two months and put them in another private foster home.

Geddes' initial action was one of 'Prohibiting totally unsuitable private foster parents and limiting the numbers of placements in others' (Geddes, 1990, p6). One outcome was a decline in the number of private fosterings in Swindon as, Geddes suspected, parents began to use private foster homes in neighbouring authorities where the SSDs had less involvement with private fostering. He then visited the private foster homes regularly and built up positive relationships with some private foster parents. Not least, he made contact with some natural parents and was able to mediate between them and the foster parents.

In Lambeth, it was acknowledged that there were a number of 'old-style' private foster homes where the parents did not visit and where the foster parents resented any contact with social workers. However, a specialist private fostering officer developed a scheme whereby private foster parents were partly paid from the prevention budget, where they agreed to work closely with the social worker, and where the social worker encouraged the natural parents to visit frequently. Three kinds of cases were identified:

- Where a stressed parent placed a child in order to have a short break.
- Where a parent, with no relatives or friends to help, had to enter hospital in an emergency.
- The children of West African students.

The Lambeth social worker felt that the small, experimental scheme succeeded because the social worker was able to offer practical help: fees; safety equipment, advice on welfare benefits, to the foster mothers. Unfortunately, the scheme did not become a permanent feature (Lambeth SSD, 1986).

Perhaps the most disturbing conditions of private foster children were found by social workers in Warwickshire. In 1989, they noticed an increase in numbers on a council estate in Nuneaton. As an article by Kendra Stone explained, 'When the Nuneaton north team began investigating what it thought were a few isolated cases of private fostering, it discovered a thriving network built up by two "baby brokers"' (Stone, 1990). The 30 children were all West African and drawn mostly from one tribe in Nigeria. However, their parents were not necessarily students. A slump in the Nigerian economy led some middle class Nigerians to decide that their children would be best brought up in Britain. They therefore came to Britain on a short term visit and left their children.

Social worker Stuart Rees was worried on the following grounds as quotations from the article show:

Two children were residing in a house where other children had been previously removed following abuse ... One child was found with a family where a young girl had been sexually abused ... Another family, included a schedule one offender, and had six black children in a two-bedroomed flat.

Once alerted to the influx of private foster children, the social workers found that their powers under the Foster Children Act (1980) were limited. Few private foster parents informed the SSD that they were intending to take children so it was not possible to prohibit intended placements. After visiting foster families, the SSD did issue requirements about the suitability of the foster parents and the premises. However, rarely were steps taken to remove children even if the requirements were not put in place. The reason was that the social workers considered it difficult to provide concrete evidence about unsuitability of people or premises which would stand up in court.

The African Family Advisory Service

The Nuneaton team also turned for advice to the African Family Advisory Service (AFAS). By 1981 the work of the CSCS had collapsed. It was taken over by the Save the Children Fund in a project which became the AFAS in 1985 and which soon established itself as the leading agency in the field of private fostering. It offered a training and consultancy service about private fostering to local authorities. It argued that the decreasing number of private fosterings recorded by government bodies reflected a lack of action by local authorities and not a real decline. It monitored the number of children advertised in *Nursery World* and in 1989 reported a fourfold increase over a four year period. It showed that there was not a dramatic decline in the number of West African students in Britain. It also confirmed that some Nigerians were bringing their children to Britain and then leaving them with foster parents while they returned. The danger was that contact between the natural parents and their children could be lost with the result that SSDs sometimes had to receive the children into public care. In a number of cases, AFAS workers went to Nigeria to seek information about children in order to help courts and SSDs make decisions about them.

The AFAS was not implying that most natural parents abandoned their children. On the contrary, many did visit and, as in the 1970s, there continued to be examples of conflict between parents and foster parents. For instance, an illegal immigrant from Nigeria gave birth to a baby girl after her husband had left her. She placed her daughter with foster parents and, after a while, stopped visiting. The foster parents then wanted to adopt the girl while the mother decided she wanted to return to Nigeria with her. The judge ruled that to go back to a Nigerian culture with a mother she did not know was not in the child's interests and that the adoption proceedings should continue. The mother was later served with a deportation order. In such cases, AFAS was prepared to advise natural parents and to try to get the courts to consider what it would be like for African children to be brought up in a basically white and European culture.

The Children Act (1975) had legislated for custodianship orders. They came into effect in December 1985. Section 33 allowed any person to apply to a court for a custodianship order concerning a child who had been living with them for 12 months providing they had the consent of the person who had the legal custody of the child, and to do so after three years without consent. Custodianship bestowed parental rights and duties on the carers so that they, not the natural parents, made the decisions about where the children lived, where they were educated, what medical treatment they received and so on. Unlike adoption, a custodianship order could be revoked by the court and unlike adoption it did not remove the legal relationship with the child's birth parents. AFAS anticipated that many private foster parents would seek custodianship.

In fact, subsequent research found that custodianship orders had little impact. A study made at Bristol University established that over half the applicants were grandparents with a typical case being where a single mother had left her child with her parents. Only a third of the children were in care. Only a handful of applicants were non-relatives like private foster parents. The researchers concluded that many of the people looking after the children were ignorant of the legislation, that some did not want to upset their relationship with the natural parents by going to court, while others wanted adoption because it could not be revoked (Bullard and Malos with Parker, 1990). The AFAS prepared and distributed literature about custodianship orders and was prepared to help natural parents involved in court cases. However, their services were not in great demand and custodianship was run-down following the Children Act (1989).

The Children Act (1989)

As in every decade since the 1940s, the 1980s witnessed major debates about services for children in public care or likely to enter care as a prelude to child care legislation. The major child care reports of the time, however, said little about private fostering. The Barclay Report was set-up to consider the roles and tasks of social workers and contained much discussion about how child care social workers could work with local communities. But its only significant comment on private fostering was to say that 'The private fostering favoured by West Africans is not yet adequately supported and protected by legislation and a clearly defined role for social workers in this area of cross-cultural fostering is urgently needed' (National Institute for Social Work, 1982, para. 9.54). The House of Commons Social Services Committee conducted an investigation, chaired by Renee Short MP, which advocated much greater emphasis on preventative work by local authorities but it did not even mention private fostering (House of Commons, 1984).

None the less, information about private fostering, as outlined in the early part of this chapter, was surfacing. It showed that:

- The numbers of private foster children were far greater than those notified to local authorities.
- Many West African children were placed by their London-based parents on estates in southern and western England.
- West Africans were not the only kind of private foster children.
- Many were in unsuitable homes.
- Few SSDs or SWDs were engaged with private fosterings while, those that were, often considered that they could not take effective action.

During the 1950s and 1960s such information and pressure on the government to act had come from ACO and ACCO. By the 1980s, BASW and the ADSS took much less interest and it was left to AFAS and individuals to do the lobbying.

The AFAS made four major recommendations:

1. That local authority practice should change so that they stopped unsuitable placements before they started.
2. That, as in Scotland, natural parents should have a duty to inform of placements before they were made.

3. That local authorities should strictly limit, and enforce, the number of private foster children taken by foster parents. It cited a case where nine private foster children were with one family.
4. That social workers be equipped by training to give more attention to the needs of black foster children.

In February 1989, while a new Children Bill was before parliament, I wrote a letter to the press in which I argued that local authorities should have a duty to visit private foster children at least once a month; that they should be obliged to visit natural parents to inform them about the condition of their children and, if necessary, to encourage more contact between them and their children; that they be empowered to provide support and training to private foster parents. But discussion in the Commons about private fostering was minute compared with the time given to that about children in public care.

The ensuing Children Act (1989) was the most important and comprehensive child care statute since 1948. Its 108 sections dealt with the concepts of the welfare of the child and parental responsibility, laid down the rules and principles for family proceedings within the courts, established new care and supervision orders and much more. Part III of the Act dealt with 'Local Authority Support for Children and Families' with Section 17 saying it was the duty of every local authority 'to safeguard and promote the welfare of children within their area who are in need' and empowering local authorities to provide them with services.

What of specific private fostering legislation? Part IX of the Act covered 'Private arrangements for fostering children.' The definition remained much the same, namely that a privately fostered child was one:

under the age of 16 and who is cared for, and provided with accommodation by someone other than: (i) a parent of his; (ii) a person who is not a parent of his but who has parental responsibility; (ii) a relative of his. (Section 66)

The section added that in the case of a child who is disabled, the age is under 18. The section also made clear that a child is not privately fostered if the person looking after them has done so for less than 28 days.

Section 67 stated that it was the duty 'of every local authority to satisfy themselves that the welfare of children who are privately fostered within their area is being satisfactorily safeguarded and promoted and to secure that such advice is to those caring for them as appears to the authority to be needed.' It also empowered the Secretary of State to make regulations imposing requirements to be met by the officials when carrying out this duty. The same section also stated that when a local authority was not satisfied with the welfare of a privately fostered child, it could take steps to ensure that the care of the child was undertaken by a parent or a relative.

In line with previous legislation, Section 68 listed the grounds under which persons were disqualified from taking private foster children unless they had obtained written consent from the local authority to do so. Section 69 made clear that a local authority could prohibit any intended or actual fostering where they considered the foster parents or the premises to be unsuitable. The foster parents had the right to appeal to a court against such action or against other actions listed above.

Schedules 7 and 8 of the Act also dealt with private fostering. Schedule 7 stated that, unless the local authority made an exemption, a foster parent could not take more than three children. Schedule 8 explained that a local authority could impose conditions on private foster parents such as the number, age and sex of the children and the standard of accommodation and equipment. Not least, the schedules extended Part IX to cover children under 16, who were pupils at schools not maintained by a local authority and who lived at the school for more than two weeks during the school holidays. Again, the local authority had powers to exempt schools. This provision brought England and Wales in line with the Scottish legislation of 1984.

The Guidance and Regulations

The Children Act (1989) deserves credit for giving precise meaning to the definition of a private foster child and a greater clarity to the duties of local authorities. The powers of local authorities regarding the circumstances in which they could prohibit a placement were fully spelt out. There is one other important aspect. The Act empowered the Secretary of State to issue regulations about private fostering, with particular mention of the requirement that the natural parents notify the local authority of any intending placement. Following the act of 1980, the Secretary of State had not used his powers to issue regulations. Now they soon came. The Department of Health issued *The Children Act 1989. Guidance and Regulations. Volume 8. Private Fostering and Miscellaneous* (hereafter called the Guidance and Regulations) in 1991 and they soon came into effect. The volume started by explaining that the new Act superseded that of 1980 and that local authorities 'will need to review their existing policies and practice in the light of the regulations and guidance and give the same priority to these responsibilities as to other statutory duties' (Department of Health, 1991, piii). In other words, local authorities were exhorted to have as great a concern for private foster children as those in public care or 'looked after' by them to use the new term.

Further, the introduction made clear that the local authorities general duty 'to safeguard and promote the welfare of children within their area who are in need' (Section 17) could include potential or actual private foster children who were thus entitled to services for 'in need' children. It was made clear that the parents of such children could be serviced in order to prevent them having to put their children in private foster homes while private foster carers (as they were increasingly called instead of foster parents) could receive services in order to improve the quality of care they provided. The regulation thus resolved the previous lack of clarity about whether public funds could be spent on the private fostering participants.

Despite underlining the statutory obligations of local authorities towards private foster children, the volume was also at pains to distinguish between them and local authority foster children. It emphasised that the natural parents selected the foster homes and that 'The role of local authorities is to satisfy themselves that the arrangements are satisfactory and that the foster parents are suitable. *They do not approve or register private foster parents.* A proper balance, therefore, needs to be maintained between parental private responsibilities and statutory duties towards private foster children' (Department of Health, 1991, para. 1.1.5).

The Guidance and Regulations emphasise the importance of notifications. They make clear that any person intending to foster a child 'is required to notify the local authority not less than six weeks and not more than 13 weeks before he receives the child' (Department of Health, 1991, para. 1.6.1). The only exception is in an emergency when notice has to be given within 48 hours of the placement. In addition, foster carers had to notify any subsequent changes in their address. Then came a statement for which several people concerned about private fostering had lobbied. It stated, 'The Act places a new duty on any parent, or person with parental responsibility for a child, to notify the local authority in whose area the child is proposed to be privately fostered' (para. 1.6.16). Given the importance of notification, the Guidance and Regulations add that local authorities had to devise 'an efficient notification system' and make known the requirement to notify (para. 1.6.20).

Once they know of the existence of private foster children, then local authorities can use their quite considerable powers. Some mention of these powers as laid down in the Act itself have already been mentioned. The Guidance and Regulations draw them together to show that they can act immediately to ban disqualified persons, can prohibit persons where they are of the opinion that they are 'not a suitable person . . . the premises are not suitable' (Department of Health, 1991, para. 1.8.22), can make requirements of the private foster carers to make improvements, and, in extreme cases, where the child may be suffering 'significant harm', can apply for an emergency protection order or a care order in order to remove a child as provided for in Part V of the Act. All actions taken against the carers can be appealed against in the courts.

The Guidance and Regulations also stipulate how frequently officials should visit private foster children, make some provision for after-care, advise social workers to facilitate contact between natural parents and their children and also discuss good practice. These matters will be taken up in the last chapter.

Comprehensive child care legislation for Scotland followed in the Children (Scotland) Act of 1995. Its wide-ranging sections dealt with the responsibilities of parents and insisted that the views of children had to be taken into consideration. It laid down the provisions for children in care (now called 'looked after children') and made reforms to the children's hearings system and so on. Its Section 22 about children 'in need' was akin to Section 17 in the 1989 Act, adding that any services should have regard to each child's 'religious persuasion, racial origin and cultural and linguistic background.' The Foster Children (Scotland) Act of 1984 had already laid down the foundations for private foster care and the new Act made just a few minor alterations.

The Children Act (1989) and the Children (Scotland) Act (1995) still stand as the legislation which largely shapes child care practice in England, Scotland and Wales. For private fostering in England and Wales, the specific private fostering legislation within the 1989 Act, combined with the ensuing Guidance and Regulations, provide a comprehensive guide to the powers, duties and practices of all private fostering participants. Apart from being the most detailed approach to private fostering ever published, the legislation is also noteworthy for the following reasons:

- It placed a duty upon natural parents to notify local authorities of intended placements. This duty not only increased the chances that notifications might be made, it also served as a statement that local authorities wanted to work in partnership with the parents.
- By placing a usual limit of three private foster children with any carers, the government made clear that it was prepared to tackle the danger of overcrowding and, indeed, of baby-farming.
- By specifying the number of visits to be made by social workers to private foster children, the message went out to local authorities that private foster children could not be ignored for months or years on end and that they required regular inspection as much as local authority foster children.
- Both the Act and the Guidance and Regulations gave particular attention to the needs of children from ethnic minorities.
- Local authorities were given some new powers to provide after-care services for former private foster children.
- For the first time, provision was made for local authorities to spend money to assist private foster parents in their tasks and, in some cases, to facilitate contact between natural parents and their children. For private foster children deemed to be 'in need', they and their carers were entitled to receive the kind of local authority services available to other children 'in need'.

The new legislation was not without its limitations and its critics. The private fostering lobby was quick to say that the legislation had not grasped the nettle of giving local authorities the power to register or approve any private foster parents before any placement could be made. Again, some pointed out that the Guidance and Regulations offered little useful guidance on just how local authorities could ensure that notifications were made. Not least, the legislation made no provision for earmarked resources for SSDs and SWDs so that they could fully carry out their obligations. None the less, the Children Act (1989) does stand out as a milestone in the history of private fostering. As a later report by the Race Equality Unit put it, 'The 1989 Children Act brings private fostering into the mainstream of children's legislation, and recognises that the nature of the experience for the child is the same in private fostering as in local authority care' (Race Equality Unit, 1993, p8).

Throughout the 1980s, private fostering remained a shadowy area with many local authorities doing little to seek out and help private foster children. Yet the decade ended with the most comprehensive private fostering legislation to date. Why? One reason is that it came in on the tails of legislation about children in care and 'at risk'. Any major overhaul of child care legislation, like that of 1948, had to include private fostering if for no other reason than it was a statutory responsibility. But the pressure for and the direction of change came not from any politicians who crusaded for private fostering. Instead it came from a handful of statutory social workers and the small voluntary body AFAS.

The Acts of 1984 and 1995 in Scotland and of 1989 in England and Wales did give notice that private foster children were of importance and provided local authorities with the duties and powers to take action. The questions for the 1990s were whether:

- SSDs and SWDs would respond.
- Their social workers would give more priority to private foster children.
- Departments would be proactive in seeking out private foster homes.
- They would take the initiative to establish practices which natural parents and private foster carers would deem useful.

Chapter 5: The 1990s and the Re-emergence of Private Fostering

The Children Act (1989) and the Children (Scotland) Act of 1995 seemed to usher in a new era in child care. What of private fostering? Despite the sections on private fostering in the Act of 1989 and the publication of the Guidance and Regulations, central government interest was at a low ebb in the early 1990s. Indeed, in 1991 the Department of Health stopped collecting and publishing statistics on private fostering with the Scottish Office following suit soon afterwards. The Chief Inspector of the Social Services Inspectorate explained, 'The collection of statistics on private fostering was discontinued in 1991 because there were serious doubts about the reliability of the information' (Social Services Inspectorate, 1997). It appeared that something was amiss with SSDs if they were not providing reliable information about private fostering. But something was also lacking at central government level if it reacted by simply ceasing to issue statistics rather than by ensuring that local authorities provided reliable figures.

The real explanation seemed to be that top figures in both central and local government regarded private fostering as a diminishing problem which was set to disappear and to which busy SSDs and SWDs could safely give little attention. Yet Frances Rickford drew upon research by Save the Children Fund which estimated that West African private foster children alone numbered 5–9,000 at this time. She summed up in 1992, 'Despite new duties and powers under the Children Act most authorities have hardly begun to get to grips with the situation and the majority of children are still unknown to local social services' (Rickford, 1992).

The Social Services Inspectorate

Despite the low priority given to private fostering by SSDs and SWDs, a handful of social workers, health visitors and race relations workers did develop their concern about private foster children. Similarly, a few middle level government officials, particularly within the Social Services Inspectorate, did not want to lose the opportunities created by the new legislation to focus on the topic. Between them, they managed to focus some attention on private fostering which came to fruition in three publications in the mid 1990s.

The Race Equality Unit of the National Institute for Social Work, headed by Bandana Ahmad, drew together *Black Children and Private Fostering*. It accused local authorities of not using their powers to deem private foster children as being 'in need', of failing to prohibit unsuitable placements, of ignoring the trans-racial aspects of many private fosterings, and not providing the resources to support natural parents, private foster children and private foster carers. In short, it declared that local authorities were content with 'a second class service ... (which) has failed children who are privately fostered' (Race Equality Unit, 1993, p13).

The momentum created by the report was maintained by the Social Services Inspectorate which, in 1993–94, examined what SSDs were doing about private fostering in three local authorities. Their findings were published as a pack in 1994 entitled *Signposts. Findings from a National Inspection of Private Fostering.* Within the first SSD which was inspected, the inspectors noted that it had 'no developed procedures, no publicity material, and the subject of private fostering had not been addressed in staff training' (SSI, 1994, p4). The second department did have a written policy and procedures about private fostering but had only two cases both of which were well supervised by social workers. However, the inspectors considered that more private fostering was going on than the department knew about.

The third SSD had 46 private foster children with 29 carers. It had well developed policies, procedures and staff training relevant to private fostering. It had distributed publicity material about private fostering and the department offered free membership of the National Foster Care Association to private carers. The inspectors' main concern was about Nigerian children being placed in white rural areas. They wrote, 'The carers appeared to have little or no knowledge of the culture these children were coming from and seemed unaware of the implications for the children of being placed in white rural families. They were also unaware of the issues relating to parental responsibility and parental participation and some actively discouraged family contact'. The inspectors continued that the social workers were working hard to promote better practice but 'it appeared that many parents were anxious and suspicious about the involvement of the local authority in the placement' (SSI, 1994, p6).

Overall, the inspectors noted that the requirement to notify local authorities of placements was virtually unknown to the general public. This 'appeared to result in significant under-notification, and could mean that there are large numbers of potentially vulnerable children in placements without any monitoring whatsoever' (SSI, 1994, p2). They were also worried that some managers and staff were not conversant with private fostering legislation.

At the same time as its above work, the Social Services Inspectorate also financed the African Family Advisory Service, through its parent body Save the Children, to undertake a study in three more local authorities. It concentrated on three SSDs, Hampshire, Kent and Shropshire, which were known to have higher numbers of private foster children than most other departments. The study, *Private Fostering. Development and Practice in Three English Local Authorities* was not published until 1997, by which time the work of the AFAS had come to an end.

Hampshire was studied because it 'had witnessed a huge growth in private foster care for West African children on particular housing estates in the Havant and Petersfield areas' (AFAS, 1997, p13). In Havant, the Family Placement Panel was given responsibility for assessing the suitability of private fostering arrangements and for issuing requirements and prohibitions where necessary. The SSD then initiated a team to 'target' private fostering with a specialist social worker of West African ethnicity to co-ordinate their efforts. A close working relationship was formed with the Nigerian High Commission. On the estates, meetings were established for groups of private foster carers.

The intentions of the SSD did not always come to fruition. At ground level, resources were still short with priority given to the statutory foster homes. Numbers of the private foster carers were hostile to and unco-operative with the social workers. Most notifications continued to be made after the children arrived in the private foster homes so pre-placement assessments of their suitability could not be made. In practice, it also emerged that 'the effort required to prohibit fostering once a placement was underway was prodigious' (AFAS, 1997, p19). The social workers found that the care provided in some private foster homes was well below that which social workers would accept in a local authority home but was not sufficiently poor to justify legal proceedings. This particularly applied if the natural parents were likely to say they were satisfied with the placement and if the private foster carers said they were experiencing no problems with the children. Moreover, when the SSD did initiate proceedings, the child was likely to be moved quickly to another foster home.

Notwithstanding these hurdles, the Hampshire social workers had striven to safeguard the private foster children and the report recorded that its SSD rightly 'came to be regarded as a flagship for developments in the supervision of private fostering arrangements' (AFAS, 1997, p13). The staff wanted to be more effective and regretted that the 1989 legislation 'had not imposed a form of registration of the carers by the local authority before which it would be unlawful for a prospective foster parent to undertake a first placement without an assessment' (p19).

Kent had also experienced a groundswell of private fosterings with most being scattered in enclaves in the district of Thanet. The study found that 'none of the private foster homes in the area had been visited routinely by social workers in the previous 3–5 years' (AFAS, 1997, p21). This deficiency was attributed to priority being given to the supervision of children in public care and to an increase in child protection investigations. The SSD did have a draft policy statement on private fostering, although it was limited to saying that it would fulfil its responsibilities and did not elaborate on means and methods. However, the SSD was proposing to appoint private fostering project officers in its five areas.

Shropshire had witnessed an even more recent arrival of private foster children, particularly on isolated council estates. In 1991, feeling overwhelmed by the demands of the recent child care legislation, the SSD had not developed a policy on private fostering. It then faced a number of child protection cases linked with West African private foster children. In one instance, a Nigerian private foster child caused concern at school and was also stealing. The private foster carers told the social worker that they wanted rid of him but his parents did not keep an appointment to collect him. A court hearing was fixed for care proceedings but the boy disappeared. Such cases prompted the SSD to extend the remit of its Family Placement Working Group to cover private fostering.

The study of the three SSDs led the researchers to identify a number of common issues. One was that the notification system was ineffective so that there was a serious under-reporting of private fostering. Another was that black children not only suffered early separation from their parents but also, where little contact was maintained between them, also suffered the effective loss of their culture, religion, language and a sense of pride in their own race. Not least, the authors noted that the social workers had little knowledge about and contact with the natural parents, partly because they tended to live a considerable distant from the private foster homes. Consequently there was little discussion with the parents and little joint planning for the children's futures.

The study concluded with three main recommendations:

1. That consideration be given to a system of registering private foster carers so that natural parents had to find a private placement from the approved list kept by the local authority.

2. That partnerships had to be developed amongst the key players in private fostering. Social workers had to enter into partnerships with the natural parents both to advise them about the suitability of proposed placements and also to help them to negotiate with the carers about how their children would be looked after. Social workers also needed to work closely with private foster carers so that the latter would find positive gains from involvement with the local authority. Social workers and health visitors also needed closer partnerships for, although the social workers had statutory responsibilities for private foster children, it was often the health visitors who had better access to young private foster children and more cordial relationships with private foster mothers,

3. Particular attention had to be given to the needs of black children placed with white foster carers. The researchers pointed out that the Guidance and Regulations which followed the Children Act (1989) made specific reference to these needs.

The two studies had similar findings and recommendations. They agreed that notifications of private fosterings were but a tip of a numerical iceberg, that a network of private foster arrangements existed on some estates, that private foster children were moved around too frequently, that, although some children received satisfactory care, the overall standard of care was below that for other children. They noted that some SSDs were not pursuing their obligations towards private fosterings while others were demonstrating good practice. But even amongst the latter, social workers tended to have little contact with natural parents and felt restricted in the control they could extend over and the help they could give to private fosterings.

The reports did receive coverage in the national press. They reflected the high point of official interest in private fostering in the early 1990s. But it was a high point which was like a molehill compared with the mountain of interest in other aspects of child care. There followed another trough during which few MPs and civil servants even mentioned private fostering.

The British Agencies for Adoption and Fostering

When AFAS published its report in 1997, the British Agencies for Adoption and Fostering (BAAF) issued a press release. It stated that, of the placements notified to local authorities, 'almost all gave room for improvement and many gave rise to concern. There were many examples of foster carers having no understanding of the children's culture and ethniciity, treating them like 'toys' and offering little support against racist attitudes, occurring even in their own homes' (BAAF, 1997). BAAF had made its mark in the advancement of adoption under its earlier name of the Association of British Adoption Agencies. It then took greater interest in local authority fosterings while, under its able director, Felicity Collier, it gave more attention to private fostering. BAAF had been consulted by AFAS about the study and, once AFAS folded, it was BAAF which took up the flag for private fostering.

It was BAAF which initiated, in the early 1990s, the Private Fostering Practice Issues Group in order to bring together social workers, health visitors, academics and occasionally, government officials. Under the leadership of Peter Wrighton and Maria Spencer, the group has enabled members to identify and discuss private fostering matters. Just as important, it has offered support and encouragement to social workers and health visitors whose concern about private fostering was often not given resources by their employers.

One of the prominent members of the Private Fostering Practice Issues Group was Beverley Clarke who chaired a group of health visitors known as the Private Fostering Special Interest Group of the Health Visitors Association. This group, in conjunction with BAAF, compiled a guide for private foster carers called *Caring for Other People's Children. A Guide for Private Foster Carers* (Batty, (Ed.) 1995). It was designed to help foster carers and particularly private carers with black children. After outlining the legislation relating to private fostering, the booklet had an important section on 'How children feel about themselves'. Its essence was that black children moving into a white family were also undergoing the difficult and probably painful experience of moving from one culture to another. In order to preserve and develop their sense of identity, the authors offered practical advice. They urged the foster carers to ensure that the children knew about their parents' own customs, to respect their religion and names, to facilitate contacts with other black people, and to protect them from and help them to cope with racism. Most of the rest of the booklet was about health, about dietary needs, skin and health care, circumcision, sickle cell disorder, hepatitis infection, HIV infection and AIDS.

A year later BAAF published a companion guide for natural parents who were considering putting their children with private foster carers called *Your Child and Foster Care*. Parents were urged to contact the local SSD to see if they knew any reason why these carers should not be used. Once the children had moved in, the booklet stressed the vital importance of maintaining regular contact by visits, letters and phone. It warned parents about the danger of foster carers applying for custody or adoption of foster children with whom the parents had not maintained strong links and added that such cases 'show how important it is for parents to keep in touch with children who are in foster care, and also the importance of telling your child and the carer about the future plans that you have for your child' (Batty and Wrighton, 1996, p9).

In 1998, BAAF issued yet another publication, a study by Lynda Ince about the experiences of black children in public care. It included a case history of a Nigerian girl called Marcel, who was 18 at the time she was interviewed, having come to England some 11 years before. She lived with white private foster carers before a local authority gained care and control over her. Marcel said to the researcher, 'I don't see myself as a black person and I don't see myself as a white person' (Ince, 1998, p75). As Frances Rickford pointed out in *The Guardian*, the study lent weight to those who advocated the need to place black children with black carers and she questioned the position of the health minister, Paul Boateng, who had tended to dismiss this approach as that of politically correct, trendy social workers (Rickford, 1998).

The Private Fostering Practice Issues Group and the publications of BAAF succeeded in stimulating more interest in private fostering and in November 1998 BAAF organised what was probably the first major conference on private fostering in Britain. Entitled *A Very Private Practice*, it was addressed by Iris Amoah, previously a social worker for the Nigerian High Commission, by Yvonne Martins, African social worker in Newham who had previously been a private foster child herself, and by Angus Geddes, who spoke about his extensive experience as a local authority social worker who specialised in private fostering. These speakers appear later as interviewees in this book. Another speaker was Marian Stuart, a senior civil servant with the Department of Health who had been a member of the team supporting Sir William Utting in his review of safeguards for children of which more will be said below. Pam Robinson, assistant director in Portsmouth SSD and previously principal advisor in child care in Hampshire, spoke about some of the positive policies and practices of SSDs in the realm of private fostering.

A powerful talk came from Joy Okoye, a barrister who spoke on 'The Lawyer and Private Fostering: A Black Perspective'. She often represented natural parents of West African foster children who had lost, or who were in danger of losing the custody of their children to white carers. She pointed out that Section 8 of the Children Act (1989) gave courts considerable powers to make orders, particularly residence orders, whereby non-relatives could get custody over children once a child had lived with them for three years. Okoye argued that in law the paramountcy of birth parents was established but that in practice much hostility was expressed towards black parents. She was worried that judges too often regarded the placement by African parents of their children with other carers as an abandonment of their children and that reports made to and decisions made by courts too often reflected Eurocentric rather than African standards. She added that West African parents were often poorly represented in court and that they were unable to express their views in a manner which the judiciary found acceptable.

The conference was a landmark in that it attracted local authority and voluntary social workers, health visitors, paediatricians and academics. More articles on private fostering appeared in the newspapers. A TV documentary on Channel 4 called *Black Bag* appeared in 1997 and, following the conference, a radio programme in November 1998. A few articles, a TV and a radio programme hardly entail massive publicity but they did reflect more interest than in previous years. The improvement was due largely to BAAF taking up the cause of private foster children. In the second half of the twentieth century, legislation placed increasing duties about private fostering onto local authorities. Yet much of the credit for keeping the topic before the public must go to three voluntary bodies, the CSCS, AFAS and BAAF.

The Utting Report

The effect of BAAF's campaigning must not be exaggerated. In Scotland, studies of private fostering had been even fewer than in the rest of Britain. In 1998–99, I explored the possibility of a survey amongst Social Work Departments with a view to identifying their involvement with private foster children. My initial letters to the major departments met with the response that they had very few known private foster children. Aberdeen reported that it had four, Dundee two, Edinburgh 12, Glasgow four and so on. The officials who replied indicated that the numbers were obviously under-reported. One department stated that it had stopped collecting information about private fostering and that my letter was a reminder that they should do more. I approached the Scottish Social Work Services Group, which was inviting applications for child care research grants. My application was immediately given the lowest priority in the rankings of child care research importance. It is worth noting that David Berridge, in his review of fostering research, summarises numerous pieces of research concerning the fostering of children by local authorities. The only recent published piece of research in the 1990s he could find about private fostering was the small study already mentioned by AFAS (Berridge, 1997). Yet, despite the absence of studies, research bodies still did not think that private fostering was worth investigation.

The inactivity of local government in England, Wales and Scotland reflected that of central government. During these years, the annual reports of the government's Chief Inspector of the Social Services Inspectorate cover a host of child care matters but not private fostering. In 1998 the government launched its Quality Protects programme to transform the quality of care for looked after children and children in need (Department of Health, 2000a). Yet, as Felicity Collier pointed out, the Quality Protects schemes were 'silent' about private fostering (Collier, 1998).

Again, 1998 witnessed the start of a national foster carers recruitment campaign overseen by the National Foster Care Association, the Association of Directors of Social Services, and the Local Government Association. Private foster carers were not included. The same year saw the long awaited publication of National Standards for Foster Care but these were not applied to private fostering. In the year 2000, the government announced the setting up of a Children's Fund whose coverage would include preventative work with 'hard-to-reach' groups. From what the government has stated, potential and actual private foster children are not in the frame.

Yet private fostering was highlighted in one important official report. These years were marked by much public concern about the abuse, especially the sexual abuse, of children separated from their own families. The government set up a review of the safeguards for vulnerable children in England and Wales (with a similar review in Scotland). It was undertaken by Sir William Utting in conjunction with others and was published in 1997 as *People Like Us*. It considered and made recommendations about children in children's homes, local authority foster care, boarding schools and residential schools. Significantly, Utting also looked into private fostering. He noted that a few local authorities had tried to raise awareness of private fostering regulations but with little success with some private carers remaining ignorant of the regulations while others just flouted them. He continued:

This is not a situation that can be tolerated. These must surely be amongst the most vulnerable of children living away from home. They may be placed at a very early age, sometimes, it seems, without contact with their parents, or anyone else with a responsibility for their welfare, for a number of years.
(Department of Health and the Welsh Office, 1997, para. 3.78).

Utting outlined three options:

1. Leave matters as they were: but all the evidence was that this put children at risk.

2. Deregulate on the grounds that the private fostering regulations were unenforceable. He rejected this on the grounds that it 'would be a honey pot for abusers frustrated as a result of safeguards elsewhere in the system' (para. 3.79).
3. To introduce a system of registering private foster carers.

Utting favoured the third option but, as I will explain in more detail in the last section of the book, the government refused to implement this recommendation and instead promised a private fostering awareness campaign in 1999.

The government did not, as promised, take action in 1999. In June 2000 the Chief Inspector of the Social Services Inspectorate, Denise Platt, wrote to all councils and referred to the SSI's pack *Signposts* which had appeared in 1994. She acknowledged, 'I do not believe that many councils used this material to improve their services.' She reminded them to meet their responsibilities for supervising private foster children and added that the SSI would inspect local authorities between December 2000 and March 2001 (Social Services Inspectorate, 2000). Simultaneously, the new Health Minister, John Hutton, issued a press release headed, in somewhat exaggerated terms, 'Crackdown on Private Fostering Regulations'. He stated, 'Despite the fact that legislation exists, it is evident that many councils are not complying with regulations and guidance on this matter.' He then announced, 'An awareness campaign during 2001 to encourage carers and parents to contact their local council about children being cared for' (Department of Health, 2000b).

The Utting Report, at least, did recognise private fostering as did the government's response. In Scotland, the counterpart report, *Children's Safeguards Review* (Scottish Office, 1997) and *The Scottish Office Response to the Children's Safeguards Review* (Scottish Office, 1998) did not even rate it worth considering.

New Groupings

The refusal of the government to implement the main proposal of the Utting Report suggests that central government still believed that the needs of private foster children were both small and diminishing. Chris Davies, then president of the Association of Directors of Social Services, regretted the government's lack of response to the Utting Report but then explained SSDs lack of involvement with private fostering on the grounds that, 'For SSDs, private fostering is a very small issue in terms of numbers' (Davies, 1998). Far from it. Throughout the 1990s it was becoming clear that private fostering was spreading beyond West African children. It is helpful to identify the groupings:

1. Young children placed by natural parents with private foster carers whom they select. The number of children placed by lone parents almost certainly has decreased. This is not to say it has disappeared and, for example, I came across a man, in the neighbourhood where I live, whose wife had left

him, who put his youngest daughter with neighbours so that he could continue at work. However, the bulk of young private foster children are made up of West African children, although their parents are not necessarily students. Political and economic instability in some West African states is prompting some parents to bring or send their children to private foster parents in Britain in the hope of giving them a better start in life. In Part Two of this book, I include a contribution from Moses Kollie with whom I have corresponded in Ghana. He reveals that it is not uncommon for children there to be placed with relatives and strangers in order to facilitate their schooling and vocational training. In addition, Moses' account shows how he also faced, with great fortitude, near poverty, exploitation and then being a refugee. If his parents had had the means, they might well have preferred to send him to foster parents in a European country in order to ensure his safety and education. The opportunity did come to one set of parents in the Ivory Coast, although the outcome was to be anything but safety. Adjo Victoria (known as Anna) Climbie's parents, believing she would have a better life in Europe, agreed that a great aunt, whom they had only met twice, should take her. The woman, Marie Kouao, took Anna on a false passport which stated she was her daughter and came to Britain. In London, she and her lover caused Anna's death by neglect and torture in February, 2000. Technically, Anna Climbie was probably a private foster child and a team headed by Sir Herbert Laming is now investigating her death. Her tragedy illustrates the fact that children are coming to Britain to live with strangers some of whom will be private foster parents. But their numbers are not known. It is not just West African children. Also to be included within this grouping are some Chinese children. Carol Woollard and Beverley Clarke state, 'There is also a significant number of Chinese children, most of whose parents work unsociable hours in catering, who find it practicable for their children to be cared for by others'(Woollard and Clarke, 1999, p109).

2. An increasing number of teenagers appear to be living away from their parents. My own observations have been of teenagers whose behaviour has prompted their parents to seek placement with private foster carers who may be the parents of the teenager's friend. These young people may return home although some move on to other friends. One social worker sent me some examples he was dealing with in 2001:

- A 14 year old boy living with a 21 year old friend.
- A 15 year old girl living with a friend of her mum's following physical assault by her stepfather.
- A 15 year old boy in his second private foster home, the latest one being with a woman whom his girl-friend knows.

Some runaways may also legally be private foster children. Professor Mike Stein and his colleagues conducted a survey in 1999 of over 2,000 children and young people aged under 16. They defined as runaways those who ran away from or were forced to leave their family home (or substitute care) and spent at least one night away. 11 per cent had run away mainly for reasons of family conflict, instability, violence, emotional abuse and neglect. Many stayed away for short periods but others, who stayed away with other carers for over 28 days, could come within the private fostering legislation. The researchers had not considered this connection and there seems little doubt that none of the runaways were notified to the local authorities as private foster children (Stein, 2000).

3. Refugees. In her study entitled *Separated Children Coming to Western Europe*, Wendy Ayotte states:

Many children who were evacuated from Bosnia and Herzegovina were placed in private fostering situations in European countries, unsupervised by state child-welfare agencies, and have not been reunited with their families ... separation from a child's parents, aside from the psychological impact, significantly increases a child's vulnerability to risk factors in her or his environment. (Ayotte, 2000, p59)

During the Chernobyl disaster, it is known that some Russian children were evacuated to Britain. These children are 'rescued' from crisis situations and brought to this country by small voluntary bodies and placed with private families. What then happens to them is unclear.

In addition, there are numbers of asylum seekers entering Britain. These include unaccompanied children and Peter Gilroy reports that Kent County Council is working with 1,200 children, some of whom have been taken into public care. Others, as he puts it, are placed with 'quasi relatives' who may, in fact, be private foster carers (Gilroy, 2001). Further, there are parents who come with children and then disappear. It is possible if not probable that some will have put the children in private foster homes.

Woollard and Clarke add, 'There are also overseas children who are brought over for adoption, and who, because of irregularities, have not come within the scope of being 'protected' children so are technically privately fostered' (Woollard and Clarke, 1999, p109). In these 'back-door' placements, as they are known, the prospective adopters have not given notice of their intention to adopt and so the children are not protected children under adoption law.

4. Children from abroad attending language schools, or on cultural exchanges, who are boarded out with private families for periods exceeding 28 days also come within the scope of private fostering regulations. The Utting Report noted language students as being potentially at risk. In its response, the government said it would 'draw up a Code of Practice for language schools bringing children from overseas'. It continued that legislation would be introduced 'to target the private fostering regulations

at placements . . . lasting more than 42 days' (Department of Health, 1998, para. 3.4). This curious response meant that many language schools would be freed from the regulations, as students tended to stay less than 42 days.

The shortsightedness of the government's reaction was revealed a year later by a report from the police which, in a 15 month period, uncovered 550 incidents of neglect, emotional and sexual abuse concerning language students aged 7–18. The incidents included lack of food, gross overcrowding, exposure to drugs and rape. The study, headed by officers from the Avon and Somerset Police, observed that only three of the incidents had been reported to them. The language schools making the placements for their students did not properly vet the prospective hosts while the SSDs did not seem to be involved at all. The police recorded that their investigation had been sparked off after they learned of a 12 year old boy being lodged with a known sex offender. Geoffrey Gibbs, in an article about language schools, wrote that 'officers knew of convicted paedophiles in Britain who were putting their names forward to look after students' (Gibbs, 1999). Fortunately, the government withdrew the 42 day proposal, although, apparently, less for a concern with language students and more because it was realised that all other private foster children would have been relieved from the oversight of local authorities for an additional 14 days.

5. Children at certain independent boarding schools who are placed with non-relatives during school holidays. These are often the children of parents who live abroad.

There may be other kinds of private foster children. One director of a Social Work Department told me of drug abusers who placed their children with neighbours. However, he was not sure if these placements went on for over 28 days or how frequently they occurred. What is sure is that the numbers of private foster children are far higher than those recorded when the government and local authorities last enumerated them in the early 1990s. This identification of new groupings of private foster children marks the re-emergence of private fostering as a matter of child care concern.

Part One of this book has shown that private fostering has been a continuing, if largely unknown, means of caring for children for 150 years. Official interest has waxed and, more often, waned. At least, the passing of wide-ranging private fostering legislation in 1984 and 1989, followed by comprehensive regulations did equip local authorities with wider duties, greater powers and fuller guidelines than ever before. A new approach seemed about to dawn. It never came. The publication of *Signposts* in 1994 by the Social Services Inspectorate, the Utting Report, and the government's announcement in 2000 that it was to initiate an awareness campaign, mark the three indications of interest in private fostering by the government in the period 1990–2000. But they were just drops of interest within a flood of disinterest. Fortunately, a few statutory welfare staff and voluntary agencies have insisted that private fostering is much more extensive and much more problematic than the government and local authorities acknowledge. So what is the present state of private fostering in the early years of the 21st century and what can be done to ensure the well-being of private foster children? Before answering these question, it is timely to listen to those who know more about it than any others: former private foster children, private foster carers and the professional experts.

Part 2
Private Fostering Participants Have Their Say

Chapter 6: The Former Private Foster Children

There is a large literature about children who are in the care of local authorities and who are placed in foster homes chosen by social workers. Private fostering has received little public attention, hence the title of this book, *The Unknown Fostering*. Even within the few publications about private fostering, the views and perceptions of the private fostering participants occur hardly at all. This part of the book, the longest and most important, does give a voice to them. Chapter 6 concerns nine former (and one present) private foster children: Chapter 7 has eight private foster carers (two of whom were interviewed together): and chapter 8 covers eight welfare professionals (two of whom were interviewed together) who have worked with private fosterings.

My approach was to interview the participants using a tape recorder. The transcript was then sent to the interviewees for their corrections and additions. The names of most of the former private foster children and private foster carers have been changed.

Sylvia Ackfield

Sylvia is a former private foster child and was in the same home as Roland Webb. She is now married with four daughters and nine grandchildren. She worked mainly as a dental nurse and receptionist and is now retired.

I was born in Lambeth where I had an older brother and a younger sister. The war came and I was evacuated when I was five. My sister and I went to a place for about two months. For some reason we did not stay and were put into separate homes. My brother was in another home nearby but they did not stay long and went back to our parents.

I just seemed to settle. I must have been sad at first because I can remember being taken to see the fish pond and the lady told me that I wept into it. But I just settled with auntie. I was the only child there during the war. Auntie joined the Women's Land Army and she milked the cows and she taught me to milk them. We had goats, chickens, pigs, cats and dogs. I had a rabbit.

First I went to the council school: then auntie sent me to a private school with seven or eight children. When I was too old for that, she paid for me to go to another private school. She was fond of me because I was the first one but I don't think I got away with anything. I was too frightened to be naughty.

I was never brilliant at school. I was OK at religious education because auntie's mother was very religious and she used to teach me every Sunday. Everyday I had to learn a text from the bible. We went to church and Sunday School every Sunday.

I was never allowed to mix with other children in the village. There was not a lot of time for play. Our life revolved around the animals, milking cows, taking dogs out on the common. I had to lay the table for breakfast. A strict routine. But I did not feel lonely. I had toys, a doll and a pram which I thought the world of. Auntie made me do educational things like a puzzle. She encouraged me to read. I painted.

A lot of her has rubbed off on me. I even write like her. But not her temper. You weren't allowed to scream or to limp if you had a blister. One day she was taking honey from the bee hive with a carving knife. A bee got in my hair and I screamed and the carving knife came past my ear. I don't know how it missed me. She never hit the children but she used to punish them. Later there was a little boy who kept losing his ball in the stinging nettles and auntie had to keep coming to get it out. She said, 'If that ball goes in there again, it will either stop in there or I will make you go to get it.' It did go in and she made him get it. He only had shorts on, no shirt. He got all those white bumps. She did not show affection. She did not put her arms around you. I was ashamed to cry. Even now, I don't like people seeing me cry. You were not allowed to show any emotion.

But there was another side to auntie. Whilst still very young, I was standing on the edge of the pond playing schools by myself and whilst waving my arms at the imaginary pupils, I fell in. I was afraid I would be told off for getting my clothes wet or have to stand in the corner for a couple of hours. But, when I told her, she took one look at me, burst out laughing and said, 'I hope you didn't frighten the fish'.

My parents did occasionally come to see me. Then they moved to Sheffield where my dad was stationed in the army. After they returned to London, I remember they took me to see Oklahoma at Croydon. It was one of the big events of my life. Then my parents seemed to fall out with auntie. It was something to do with the family allowance which my parents had claimed. After this, they were no longer allowed to come to the house and I had to go into Midhurst to see them.

Most evacuees went home after the war. I didn't, probably because deep down inside auntie wanted to keep me. She made the excuse to my parents that she wanted me to finish my education at the private school. They just said I could stay. I accepted it because that was my life.

After the war, she started having other children. I was mostly older than them and looked after them. They were glad to have me on their side. At times I felt sorry for them because she was so strict. She had a baby at one time and put it in the garage because it cried. She didn't have the patience for a baby. Auntie used to choose our clothes. You can imagine what kind of shoes she chose. It was unthought of for me to have a boyfriend. That would be the den of iniquity.

We used to have an official visitor after the war. We never spoke to her alone. If we had visitors, we were given strict instructions not to speak unless they spoke to us. This lady saw us altogether with auntie there. I was not unhappy. Life was hard, getting up early, no proper heating, putting goats out early in the morning in winter. I got chilblains on my hands but you were not allowed to complain.

My parents did not forsake me altogether. They continued to have some contact with me. When I visited them, I saw my sister going out and enjoying herself. By the time I was 15 I wanted to return to London. I was going to take my school certificate but my parents suddenly said they wanted me home so I did not do even that. But I think I was pushing my parents. I was getting fed up because there seemed to be no relaxation. You always had to be doing something. I was thinking, 'There's another life for me, I want it'.

I was frightened of auntie at times but I did not hate her. I suppose I loved her because I looked upon her as my mother. The strange part is that I don't remember feeling sad when I left. She had lost her dog and the night before I left she said, 'I don't know what I've done to deserve this, you're going tomorrow and I've lost the dog'. She was actually weeping. I went to Midhurst to meet my dad: she still wouldn't have him in the house.

It was so different when I got back home. I had long hair but auntie would not let me have it loose and she made me wind plaits about my head. It was so old fashioned so the first thing I did in London was to have my hair cut and have a curly perm. I used to go dancing and meet the boys. It was a completely different life. And my mother used to give me sugar in my tea. Auntie never allowed that. My parents didn't have two half-pennies to rub together. My dad went to work but he had little money. I left school and went to work in a chemists, then as a dental receptionist.

When I first came back to London, auntie sent me primroses, my favourites, wrapped in damp cotton wool. She always sent me a birthday card. We spent our honeymoon down there. After I got married, we went to see her. I would not

53

put make-up on as she would not like that. She still seemed to have this hold on me after I left. But I think our relationship was a little bit strained because I felt I had let her down in some way. When I first came to London, I used to speak like Penelope Keith. Then I spoke more London and I don't think she liked that.

Kriss Akabusi

Kriss Akabusi experienced several private foster homes as a young child. He later became an international athlete winning 11 medals at the Olympic Games, the Commonwealth Games, the European and World Championships. He has made many TV appearances and is now a well-known speaker on the subject of motivation.

My mother and father are Nigerians, Ibos. They came to Britain in the mid 1950s for education. They met on the boat and later married. My mother trained as a nurse and my father studied accountancy and international law at LSE. I was their first child born in 1958 and my brother, Riba, followed. I think I was with them early on, although I do not really know. Riba was born in 1960 and then we went to private foster homes. In 1961, my parents returned to Nigeria with us and then my mother brought us back to England and put us in a foster home in Brighton. There was an old lady who spent most of her time upstairs. Her son, or grandson, he was adolescent, looked after us. He was quite punitive. Then I think she died for we were suddenly taken away.

We went to a children's home or large foster home. It had these toy buses which you sat on and drove. I remember sitting on this bus and I couldn't believe that I was actually allowed to play. I learnt to clean my teeth for the first time so every five minutes I was away cleaning them. We were only there very briefly.

We then went to a Spanish lady in the Kings Cross area. She was very draconian, very punitive. They did not understand us African children and I didn't understand what they required of me. On more than one occasion, she made me drink my own urine. They had a girl who was obviously the favourite above my brother and I and, if she did anything wrong, we got the blame. The man was away a lot but when he came home retribution was immediate with belt and slipper. I had been brought up by my mother and father to protect my brother. One day, the man was about to beat me and I started to cry. My brother, who was really stubborn, didn't cry and he beat and beat him. I remember standing there and thinking that I should do something but I was fearful for myself. My parents were back in Nigeria but we were visited by an uncle. When he came, there was always somebody else in the room. I could not communicate. My uncle was a distant, quiet man, he was studying politics. You couldn't crawl over to him and whisper in his ear. He was very polite and

54

there would be cordial discussion then, after half an hour, he would leave. I wasn't visited by a social worker in any of the foster homes, I don't think anyone official knew where we were. In the end, I seem to remember blurting out to my uncle, 'This is horrible, I don't like it here.' I don't know if we had any marks on us but he recognised it was a problem and he rushed us out.

We went to another foster home in Southsea. The couple were quite strict but fair and friendly. They had their own and adopted children. I remember having the best Christmas I ever had there. I felt a bit different at school because I was a black kid. One day a black woman stopped me at the school gates and asked me where I came from. I said, 'Near here'. She told me that I was African and it was a shame that I couldn't speak my own language. I always knew that I was different. Other kids pointed out to me that I had very small ears, large lips and a broad nose. But you want to be socially accepted or you feel uncomfortable. Somehow, I was always different. Even later in the children's home, the fact that about ten of you get out of a minibus made you different.

Then the Biafran war happened in Nigeria in 1967. My parents were caught up in it so no money was coming across and we had to leave the foster home. My uncle took us to his home. We couldn't stay in his place as he just had a small basement flat. We were put on a train. I think my uncle put us on, and told us we would be met at Kings Cross. When we got out, the police took us. We went to a children's home in Enfield and were in the care of Islington. I was eight or nine. My brother was there, he was my constancy, there was a sort of parental instinct growing in me towards him.

The children's home was a new beginning. It was great fun. The first people there were quite draconian but, by this time, nothing could faze me. The next people were very, very loving. But there is a limit to the amount of love that can be shared by half a dozen adults with 20 kids all wanting attention and some with psychological problems. So it was difficult for them to love me in the way that I love my children. You compete for intimacy, for recognition. But I have good memories of it and I was there until I was 16. That was stability.

School was a non-event for me. In the children's home I was one of the few good kids who actually went to school. I quite enjoyed school because I liked the social interaction, chasing the girls, telling jokes, flicking pellets. But I wasn't academic. I had no structure, no discipline. I liked being the centre of attention: even getting the cane. I didn't like being hit but the boys thought you were hard. I was getting reward and recognition from my peer group.

My brother went to a different secondary school. He was studious, worked hard, did well in his exams, became a black belt at karate. Later in life he had a psychotic problem. We shared a room and I constantly got dragged back to tidy it again. He was very meticulous and every thing had to be in its position.

In 1975, I met my mum again. It was quite strange. Our bedroom was over the drive and every weekend and holidays, you'd hear cars coming to pick up the children who had mums or dads or who were being adopted. I remember thinking, 'I wonder if it will ever happen to me?' Then one day I got called into the house and told, 'Good news, a contact from Africa. Your mother is coming.' It didn't really mean anything to me. I was playing football in the garden and I remember seeing her, it was quite obviously her by her African clothes. I carried on playing football. They called us in, 'Your mum's here.' I carried on playing football. 'Your mum's here'. I walked in. 'This is your mum'. 'OK, hello'. It did not mean anything. Then she started talking to me, touching my skin. And I asked her if she had any sweets: she did. She said she'd come back the next day and would take us to some relatives. That was it. Another day she took us to a photographic session. She wanted me to put on all this Nigerian gear. I said, 'No way'. She said, 'You've got to, you're a prince.' In the end, I wore some of it. She told me she was coming back to take me home. That was the worse thing she could possibly say. I had in my mind the Tarzan and Jane image, mud huts, grass skirts, men with big chests. I said to the people at social services, 'I don't want to go to Nigeria' and they said I wouldn't have to go. There was a big conflab and my mother was deterred from taking me back and a year later I joined the army.

I was 16 and a half when I joined the army. I could have got a job but the idea of leaving the children's home, renting a flat, cooking for myself: no. By this time I was quite institutionalised. You are a boy and you go into a man's world. The army was very male-orientated, there are lots of strong male models, lots of parental guidance. Very strict rules and regulations. In the children's home, I'd got used to making my bed in a certain pattern and that's how the army made their beds so suddenly I began to shine. In the children's home, you had to polish your shoes so I knew how to do that. The things that I had to learn were punctuality, being committed, seeing something through. I took to that. I had a desire to please these other men.

The army was a turning point for my athletics. The troop sergeant was the athletics officer and he saw my talent. I won army competitions and from there went to the top.

My experiences away from my parents gave me an intense need to be accepted and recognised. Out of this has come my intense desire to achieve. I know that people get fed up with Akabusi but I had to achieve. In the army I wanted to climb up the army structure. Then sport gave me a ladder to achieve which I did with hard work and discipline. It's meant that I am comfortable in group environments: the army, sport, the media. Now I am a motivation speaker and that's a group environment.

In the personal relationships I am not so happy. We were moved so many times, my memory is of being torn from people I had become fond of. I learned never to let myself feel secure or that this was really home. Because I never learned how to give and receive in a natural way, I found it difficult in later life to be spontaneously loving with those closest to me. Everyone thinks I am so friendly but I have few really close friends. Even with my wife, whom I love very much, I hold something back. I learned that trusting people led to pain.

At least, I did have a time, perhaps 2–3 years, as a small child when I was cared for by my parents. I don't think Riba had that. He had to deal with issues a lot younger than I did. He was about ten months to a year when he went into a foster home. The going from one place to another and not knowing who you are and who you belong to must be really damaging. I was just that little bit older and I had responsibility for my brother. I couldn't give him the confidence which he required. He withdrew into himself and had a breakdown. He is alright now, medication has put him back on the straight and narrow. He's got a lovely wife.

Christianity has also been important to me. I became a Christian when I was 29 in 1987. I had led a good life and acquired much, I saw things as synonymous with success. Yet I found an emptiness in them. Just reading the bible, what Jesus had to say, I felt very challenged. I had a vivid dream which answered the questions and showed me that Jesus was my Lord and Saviour. My faith today is not what it was in 1987. I see that in the UK we have mixed up faith in Christ with a European dogma that can disenfranchise many people. I still understand that Jesus is my Lord and Saviour but I am not dogmatic any more. Now I see the flaws in myself. I recognise that God has a lot more room in his heart for people than I ever dreamed possible.

Now I am a motivation speaker. I travel the country encouraging people to step into the arena, into life, being committed to something. Eternity on earth is what you do for other people. You call your house your home but one day someone else will be in it. So life can not possibly be about that. I talk about investing in people, how people invest in me. I see that model in Christ. I see how Christ took three years and invested in a group of people. My message in motivation speaking is about focus, innovation and teamwork. What is the gift that God has given you and how you can invest that gift in those around you.

I now see myself as British in my mind set, but my culture is Nigerian. When I was younger, I couldn't divorce Englishness from Britishness. Now I see English as ethnicity. I am British by birth. It's like being in a club. But I am not English, I have no Anglo-Saxon blood in me. I am pure West African stock, that's my blood line, that's who I am. Once you accept that you have explanations for some of the things I do. Your environment plays a part and I think like an Englishman but my actions are very West African.

I went to Nigeria when I was nearly 21. I was a prince in the village. I saw that my actions were very African. I am very loud, I explain with my hands, with my eyes, I'm gregarious. In Africa, you see three or four people talking, you'd think they were having a fight, there's hand waving and laughter and that's the way they discourse with each other. People say to me, 'Slow down Akabusi, sit down, it's not your turn.' I was an oddity because I did not have the European way of discussion, of building case upon case. I was much more emotional. Now I understand that it's because it is in my genetic code, it's the way our people have learnt over the years to interact with one another. These are important things which, if they had been introduced to me earlier, I could have coped with some of the discrepancies between my mind set and what other people said. People used to look at me and think I was a black man, I would look at them and think I was white. I did not know where this rush to be the centre of attention was coming from.

I will go back to Nigeria. I've set up a charity and I'll live half the year in Nigeria. I've got a sense of responsibility. I've been here for 40 years and I've got responsibilities, I've got a wife and children. But in 2008 my girls will be 23 and 21 and I'll have done my job for them and I know I've got a job to do for my people. I am the first son in my village and there is a lot I can do there. I can build my hospitals, I can get pharmaceutical drugs, I can be a powerful catalyst for change in Nigeria. If you look at someone like Joseph in the bible, who got taken out of Canaan and rose up in Egypt: he was there for a reason. Maybe that's my story. I have always been here and it's beautiful in Egypt but it is for a reason. My mind set is to go back to Nigeria.

Iris Grant

Iris Grant was born in Africa and came to England when she was seven. From the age of nine to her late teens she lived with private foster parents. She has now made a successful career for herself.

I was born in Africa and lived with my mother for two years and then with my father until I was seven. During this period, I spent half the year with my father and half with my grandparents so I was always backwards and forwards. In 1968, when I was seven, my father brought me to England to be with my mother. At first I lived with my mother's sister for six months and then with my mother for 18 months. I did not know any English or her language so there was a lack of communication. When I was nine, I came home on the last day of school and my mother said I was going to live with some people for a month's holiday.

My mother told me they were a white couple and I thought they would be young and blond with long hair. I was disappointed when they were elderly. My mother was going to stay the night but she abruptly went back. I was upset but the next day I was fine. I never missed my mother which is quite odd but I suppose I had been backwards and forwards so it was just another place for me. After I had been there a month, they asked me if I wanted to stay with them. I said 'yes'. I had my own room, it was in the countryside, it was all very new. My mother made it clear that she did not want me back until I had finished my education.

My foster parents were retired teachers. They were very kind. They had no children of their own but they had had lots of dealings with children. I don't think they had thought the fostering through. They had watched a TV programme about the Biafran war and wanted to help. They contacted the Commonwealth Students' Children Society and fostered a child for a little while. Then they said they wanted a child on a more permanent basis. I don't know how my mum got in touch with the Society but they put her in touch with the foster parents.

I started in a small school where I was the only black child. I was the only black child in the town all the time I was there. There was a mixed race child in the town but I never spoke to her and she went to the secondary modern while I went to the grammar school. From the age of 14, I never spoke to another black person. It was obvious that the other people did not want me mixing with their children. All the school children were invited to one another's parties and I was always excluded. I did not go to the school Christmas parties and years later I found out that parents said that if I went then their children would not go. I went to very few of the girls' homes. I never saw the father of one girl and she said, 'Oh, he doesn't like people like you'.

I was never involved in other people's lives. I never saw anybody after school or at weekends. There was no overt prejudice. I was not called names but it was understood. I did join a gymnastics club, after school, when I was 13 and went until I was 18 because that was the only way I could go out in the evening. The rest of the time I just stayed in my room. Even when I went to night school for a year, the others used to go out afterwards but didn't include me.

My foster parents, I called them auntie and uncle, never faced up to my being black. They never acknowledged that I was different. My foster father is now dead but my foster mother still will not acknowledge my problems. When I was younger, I blocked it out. As I get older, I feel I miss out on not being part of a group. We were visited by the social services twice a year until I was about 15 or 16 when it was felt that I did not need so much supervision. I do know from the correspondence to auntie that they were worried about my isolation.

The last time I saw my mother, I was 13. She had decided she wanted me back. She said it was because she could not afford to pay my fees but I know she did not pay auntie. She arranged for me to be abducted. It was all very nasty. I said I did not want to go back. She went to my father and he came over from Africa when I was 14. He said he had the intention of taking me back but I don't think he did. He said he was a businessman and had been to London at least 50 times. I just thought, 'Why didn't you see me or even know that I was fostered?' I did not want to go back and I think auntie and uncle put ideas in my head that I was getting a much better life here.

I got O levels and A levels at school. I did not really intend to go into nursing. Years later, auntie gave me some of their correspondence with the Commonwealth Students' Children Society. They spelt out that they wanted a child who would be a nurse, doctor or teacher who would go back to their own society and teach them. What they had forgotten was that once you take a child out of that society and brought it up completely differently, the child could never go back. Being a nurse was what they wanted me to be and I fulfilled their ambition because I did not want to go back to my parents.

At 18, I left home to train as a nurse. When I was 13 I made the decision that I would move away at the first opportunity. I enjoyed being away because I felt normal and accepted by my colleagues who included me in their lives. In my first place there were only four black nurses and I don't really remember talking to them. Again I was in a white, middle class world. It was the same when I moved to a large hospital in another city. It was only when I moved for further training in another hospital that I was one of many black people and I found it hard to adjust. I was African and a lot of the black people were West Indian. One had a flat to let which I did not want because it was in a dangerous street. Next thing I hear is that I don't want to be with people like my own.

I have always felt uncomfortable with black people. Even now I don't have black friends. I am comfortable with white people. I changed my name from an African sounding one to an English sounding one. I have a British accent.

As a result of being fostered, I would say that I am a very mixed-up person. It did not hit me until I was in my thirties. I have a lot of superficial friendships just as I did as a foster child. People could only like me for a certain period of the day. I am now having counselling to deal with my past. I haven't made deep relationships.

I would say that I am just a little English girl under a black skin. I can not say that I am African. I don't know what African means. It is partly my fault because I have not made a conscious effort to get in with the African community. I was talking with a black girl who had a problem and she asked me not to tell another black person because she would say, 'Oh, why did you tell her, she's an English person?' It hit home to me that even black people think I am English so they don't accept or trust me. I feel very cut off and I am in the middle: that is why I don't form relationships with anybody because I don't know what I am or who I am.

I have never been back to Africa. It is probably because I have been so afraid of being abducted there. I know it won't happen now. Recently I was talking to an African doctor who came from the same place as me. I was horrified in case he knew somebody who might know my family who might come after me. I had to get him to swear not to say anything. There is this fear that I would not get out again.

I've a lot of anger, bitterness and sadness about what has happened to me both by my natural parents and foster parents. My aunt and uncle did not think about it from my point of view. I am sick of people saying weren't my foster parents wonderful to take you in. Yes, they were but at the end of the day do you ever think what it was like for me? Inside I feel it wasn't such a wonderful upbringing socially. Educationally, yes. At the same time I have this void in my life that I don't belong anywhere. I have no family.

I feel my foster mother is my only relative. I have lived with her longer than anybody. She is very positive towards me. I am not so positive towards her but

I don't let her see that. I know she loves me very much and I know that she thinks of me as her daughter and I am her next of kin and I'll inherit everything but there is this thing in me that our relationship is based on her love towards me rather than my love towards her. I see her every six weeks, I spend Christmas and birthdays there. Outwardly I am the perfect daughter but inwardly I feel I can't love her 100 per cent until she acknowledges the difficulties I went through. It is too late now. They never sat down and discussed why is this 16 year old girl not getting invited to parties, why does she not have friends, why does she not do anything except sit in her room?

More emphasis should be on what foster parents can provide for the child emotionally. The child's background should be looked into to see how they would fit into the foster home. I don't agree that a black child should never go to a white family. But attention must be given to what the foster parents can provide for the child socially. And then children must be equipped to go out into the world. I was so isolated and my foster parents were so old. I haven't seen their nephews and nieces for 20 years because I was never considered part of the family. When auntie dies, I feel I will have nobody.

Anybody can take a private foster child to meet their own needs but they may not be meeting the child's needs. It would have been better if I had been in a place nearer to other black children or if they had acknowledged my blackness and given me some books and magazines which took into account that I am black or talked about the problems I would have to face. It is all very well to say 'we love you, we don't see colour at all.' Other people do see your blackness and you have to deal with it. Ultimately, you have to go out in the world, you have to go to school, you are going to be left in the classroom while others go out.

I have asked myself would it have been best if I had stayed with my mum? Educationally, no. No, she was not meeting my emotional needs either. She was not into me as she was into her other two children. So I have never felt connected to her either. I wouldn't have had a better life but I would probably have more sense of community and family. Even if I had not got on with my mother, I'd have been in an African community because we used to go to a Pentecostal church and my mother's sisters were a part of my life. But when I went to the foster home there was just me.

Sometimes I switch off because it is too painful and other times I think in great detail. It has held me back in relationships because I don't know who I am.

Christine Hanks

Christine Hanks went to a private foster home when she was six months old and remained until she was 22. She works for a public body as a communications assistant.

My birth parents were from Liberia. My father came to Britain to work for the embassy as an accountant and my mother followed. They left one daughter in Liberia then I was born here and then my younger sister. Apparently my father wanted my mother to work so they fostered me out in Kent. I was six months old and my sister came later when she was three weeks old.

My foster mother was a really good person. Even today, she is my mum, I don't know any other mum and we are still in touch. She looks upon us as her daughters. It must have been a struggle for her because she was a widow and had five children of her own: all much older than us.

I remember thinking that when I was five I would be taken back. That was the original arrangement which never happened and I was glad because I wanted to stay. My parents did come to see me two to three times and, once I started school, they used to come and pick us up, and my foster mum's youngest daughter, and take us to their house in London in the holidays. This continued until I was 11 or 12.

Our sister from Africa, three years older than me, was brought over and my parents wanted my foster mum to care for her as well. Also we had a social worker who was saying I ought to go back home because my foster mum's house only had two bedrooms. So my father told my foster mum that they were giving her their house in London. They brought us along with my foster mum's youngest daughter to the London house for a year. Then we moved again to Surrey because my parents had two houses and they got rid of the London one.

I did not get on very well at school, I had to go for special help with my reading. In Kent it was a white area and I was about the only black person in the school and I got bullied a lot. If we came home and said we got called names because we were black, our foster mum just said, 'Well, call them back.' She didn't know what to do. It was not that she could not be bothered, she just did not know what to tell us to do. I went to secondary school in London for a year then to one in Surrey which was again a white area. I left school with three CSEs.

A social worker used to come. Not very often. I remember our mum telling us to come straight home from school. She used to talk to me but I can't remember what about. I wondered what she wanted. I knew mum wasn't my real mum but I still did not understand why the social worker came. I never saw her alone and she never spoke to me about being black.

As a teenager I was quite naughty. I did not get into trouble with the police but I was very cheeky to my mum. I often did not go to school. After school I went to college and did a City and Guilds in community care. I had one job and then worked as an administrator. I started evening classes when I was 21 and did O levels, then an access course and on to university. I stayed with my mum until I was 22 but I used to go to London at weekends to go to night clubs. My sister moved out when she was 18 and had a baby.

I went to university and got a degree in communication. Then I did not work for two years until I got an administrative job with a charity. After a year and a half I got my present post as a communications assistant which I really enjoy.

When I was growing up, I never thought about my background and culture. It did not bother me. Now, having lived in London, I've come across a lot of black people. But there are certain things I can't do like African cooking. When friends come round I give them pie and chips. I have only recently learnt to twist my own hair but not in elaborate ways and I feel I have missed out. Sometimes I think that black people act in certain ways and I am not like that which makes me feel sad. I go to an organisation for people who have been trans-racially fostered or adopted. I wanted to meet people with whom I have something in common.

It is through private fostering that I met this woman, my mum, she's like an angel. Had that not happened I would not be the person I am today. I am very proud to be her daughter. My younger sister has turned out all right, she is quite like me. My foster family live in an all white area, which is quite far away and I would not feel comfortable living there. I rarely get to see them and, as a result, I do not have a close family structure.

My dad is back in Liberia. I don't talk to him. I don't know what he does now. I am not interested in his problems. When we were in the second house, our parents went back to Liberia and we did not hear from them for years during which time they allowed the house to be repossessed making us homeless. Then we saw our biological mother out of the blue. She thought we were still children and criticised us. But we thought she gave up that right when she put us out for fostering. So we often argued. I've cut her out, there is no point in having her in my life. My older sister went back to Africa when she was 16 and then she went to America. My biological mother followed her and works as a carer with elderly people. I have not seen her for eight years. We don't talk.

I feel anger towards my parents, my mother more than my dad. My sister in America will ring me up and tell me what my biological mother is up to and I get annoyed. She doesn't show any remorse for what they did to us, she won't talk about it. Last year I had some private counselling. I felt my life wasn't going right and I got a bit down. We used to talk about my mum and how I felt about what my parents did, how let down I felt. I was quite upset when I talked about it. I think the counselling helped me get rid of a lot of the anger.

I think private fostering should be registered because once the foster carers have got the child behind closed doors all manner of things could go on. There is no support or training for foster carers in dealing with black children. When I was little I thought that when I grew up I would be white or I'd close my eyes and think that when I opened them I'd be white. It was never explained to me why I was black. The foster children could have a week a year with other black people and learn how to do hair and so on.

Moses Kollie

From the age of 12, Moses Kollie was a foster child in West Africa.

It all started at the age of 12 in October, 1988. That was when I left my village to come to my brother, in Firestone plantation company in Liberia, who was in the low income section of the working group. I did not go with the intention of stealing but when I got there he told me to steal so that he could send me to school.

My first year with him was not pleasant at all. I attended school in bare feet. During the vacation I had to sell for my foster-parent-to-be. I was paid $15 a month and gave all the money to my brother with the intention of helping him with my fees. Unfortunately, I don't know how that money was used so my schooling for that year went from bad to worse.

It was arranged that I went to live with the woman I worked for. There I was expected to do the chores for the whole house which included washing for a family of five, including a newly born baby, do selling, and attend school. It was not an easy task at all but I was determined to learn how to read and write.

I did all these things up to July, 1989 when the war hit Firestone. My task increased from the household chores and selling to risking my life to make sure there was something on the family table. I did this up to 1992 when we crossed over to the Ivory Coast where I was made to wake up every morning at about 3.30 am to make bread for sale. I was then expected to sell the bread from 6 am to 11 am, get ready for school at 12 noon and be in school from 12.30 pm to 5 pm. When I got home at 6 pm I was expected to get all the baking material for the next morning. I did this up to 1994 when a refugee train took me to Ghana where I am now.

In Ghana I was made to help build three bedroom houses. I did not have to go out in search of food but I had to be away almost the whole day drawing water. At least I went to school but studying was another thing altogether. I did this up to 1998. When I was in my final year in senior secondary school we returned to Liberia where my foster mother turned me over to my brother whose condition had gone from bad to worse. I knew that my dream of becoming literate could come to a halt. I returned to Ghana alone and was able to successfully complete secondary school in 1998 and in 2000 I was able to learn office equipment repairs and at present I am in search of an attachment.

I think my experience as a foster child helped me to accept the war in Liberia and now I know how to read and write.

Yvonne Martins

Yvonne Martins was born in London of Nigerian parents. She was privately fostered as a baby and stayed until she was eight. She is now a social worker.

My parents were from Nigeria but had been here for some time. They were students and in 1962, when I was six months old, I was fostered with my brother who was two years older than me. I can remember being loved a lot by my foster mother, I called her 'mother'. I was the youngest child there and quite spoilt. The bond between us was very strong. My foster mother was not married but she had adopted a number of children and there were others who were privately fostered. I think she had ten in all. The house was filled with children.

Two of my foster mother's adopted daughters were close to me. They were older, probably in their early 20s and very fond of me. I was very disappointed years later when I came back to find that the one I particularly remembered had lost contact with the family.

My foster mother was very strict. We were not allowed to swear or use bad language and if that happened we had our mouths washed out with soap. But she was also very loving. She had firm boundaries about what was and was not acceptable. She used to teach me to cook and I liked to get involved. We went to church every Sunday. Her parents lived up the road and we used to visit them quite frequently.

There were not many black people in the area. One result was teasing and name calling at school because my name was Nigerian. There was an identity crisis at one stage as to who I really was. At home, the other children were used to having black children in the family. Outside it was very strange. My foster mother was very loving but when it came to the cultural aspects, she was not very aware of my needs as a black child.

She was my mother. For some reason, I didn't pick up the thing about being a different colour until later. I did not have anyone visiting and saying, 'I'm your mum. I'm your dad'. I knew there was something special about my brother but I just saw her as my mother. I must have been older than five when it dawned. It may have happened when my parents started visiting: and they then came regularly and we visited them every fortnight for a weekend and sleep over. I never liked it. I always had an illness when it was time to go. Gradually I got to know that they were my parents. I found it difficult to accept. I used to cry because I never wanted to go. Things were a bit easier for my brother because, having lived with my parents for part of his first two years, he knew that his foster mother wasn't his mother. Also he had had another private foster mother before this one. I had gone there at six months so my foster mother was the first person I had known. I didn't want to leave and that led to friction between myself and my dad.

She (foster mother) must have spoken to me about it but it was something I wasn't taking on board because I wasn't seeing anybody and because I was still living with her. There is a possibility that she may have talked to me about my birth mother and father but I did not want to take it own board.

I was eight when I left to live with my parents in London. It just happened one Sunday evening and nobody was getting ready to go back to the foster home and that was the end of it. My dad said we were not going back. My brother seemed to be OK about it but it was a bit much for me. I cried, I couldn't believe it. I kept on looking at the faces of people who I thought could be my foster mother when I was out or going to school. I don't think that my foster mother had realised I was going back for good. She knew what my parents were building up to but she never knew when it was the final time she would see us.

At first it was difficult for me to settle back with my parents because on the weekends we went back we were eating different foods, some of which we liked and some we did not. Our parents would take us out to meet Nigerian people in the community. They had children and the way they did things was a bit different from our foster mother. Our foster mother's place had been a very big house with big bedrooms, a girls' bedroom and a boys' bedroom and we had our own beds, whereas when we went to our parents it was one bedroom and there was no kitchen so my mother had to cook on part of the landing. Things became better later on when we stayed in the same house but we now had our own bedroom: my brother and myself shared a bed. Our foster mother was strict so was my real mother so there was not much difference there. The language was different for our parents spoke their native language. They would speak English to us but we knew there was another language because at times they would speak it and we couldn't understand.

When we went back to Nigeria, to Lagos, we were welcomed into the community by our grandparents and relatives. I was ten. There was a kind of novelty around it so we were treated very well. It became natural to see other black people. My dad is an accountant, my mother had learnt how to sew and made clothes. We wanted to learn the language to speak like everybody else. The language was Yoruba. There is tribalism in Nigeria, the Yoruba, the Ibo and the Hausa and a power struggle between them. The school was very different, more disciplined than in Britain. I was caned quite a few times for doing things that I shouldn't have done. We were given tests to take. If there were 34 students in the class you were given a position and because you came from overseas you were expected to be first.

Religion was a difficulty. My mother is a Muslim, my father was indifferent then he decided to become a Muslim. My foster mother had brought me up as Christian. When I first went back to my parents it was not an issue. Later, in Nigeria, it was. In my extended family there were both Christians and Muslims but by then my father had become a Muslim so there was pressure on us to become Muslims. But my brother and I decided to remain Christians.

I went to university for four years. Altogether I was in Nigeria for 12 years. Then I came back to Britain. There was an unfortunate circumstance in which my brother passed away. I'd had enough and wanted to get away. My parents were expecting me to return to Britain at some point.

I had kept in touch with my foster mum all the time, she wrote to me in Nigeria, sent photographs, told me about her grandchildren. My dad wasn't too pleased about it but he couldn't actually stop it. So I stayed with her when I went back. Everything had changed, she had changed, I had changed, her children had grown up and left home. My accent was very funny and they had a bit of difficulty understanding me. I had become accustomed to the Nigerian culture in which you had to respect certain people in certain things. It took a long time to adjust.

I worked as a nursing auxiliary with the elderly near to home and then took a similar job on the south coast. After I left the second job, I found out I could not go back home. Now I had to find my own way of life. I moved to London and had great difficulty in finding a job and was unemployed for a substantial period. Then I worked as an administrative assistant before going to a SSD as a residential social worker in a children's home with extremely difficult children. We had lots of broken windows, a mutiny at one point, they locked themselves into the kitchen. I could relate with some of the children. They liked to set off the fire alarms and fire hoses and squirt people: I did it back at one of the young people. I lasted a year and would not like to go back. But we had to learn to work together as a team in order to stay one step ahead of the young people.

I applied to be a qualified social worker which I did at university 1991–93. I then got a job with an inner London borough in their Family Placement Unit. It gave me a good grounding as I had a good supervisor. I had a little to do with private foster children. Incidentally, when I was a private foster child, we were never visited by a social worker. The private fostering cases were dealt with on a duty basis and we had a pack on private fostering so that any of us going on a visit knew what to do. The principal officer was quite open to the challenge of private fostering and there was a system in place which I have not found elsewhere. Private fostering seemed to have moved on from my own experience. It was not just black children in white families, it is now also black children in black families. Apart from students placing children, there were parents, whose children were out of control, who felt that another person, a friend, could look after them better. It is difficult for me to talk about the private foster carers because on a duty basis you visit them only once. If they knew you were coming, they could tidy up. If you did a spot check, they might not be in when you called. If you saw the children, they were with the private foster carers, you did not see them alone. Local authorities do not give private fostering the same kind of profile as they do to statutory work.

After three years, I moved to another London SSD. It seems to do little for private fostering probably because it is not pro-active because I am sure there are private foster homes. My job is as African social worker in the Teenage Fostering Team. I recruit foster carers, particularly African if we can find them. One of the things that gets me is that African children are placed in Asian families. It is done on the basis that they share a common religion, Islam. Religion is important but I think that language and culture are more important. Most of the Asian carers do not speak English, they speak their Asian language, most of them are linked with Asian social workers, and I think it is going to be confusing for a black child to be in a family where they do not know the primary language. I was a black child in a white home and I had a very difficult transition. One of the things that helped me sort out my culture was going to Nigeria. I have also been privileged in that I have been able to maintain contact with my foster mother and have a good relationship with her which is quite unique.

I don't think that private fostering should happen at all. I'd rather that black children were not put with white private foster carers but if it has to happen then I think these cases need the same kind of regulation as local authority foster carers. I was privileged in that I was not abused or anything in the family I was placed in. She was a God-fearing woman and because of that she looked after the children in her care very well. But it is not always like that. There needs to be much more contact between the children and their parents so that they know who their parents are. My parents did not visit me much in my foster home. This is something which needs to be communicated to Nigerians. It seems to be the Yoruba more than the Ibo who practise private fostering. My parents did it because they were studying at the time and did not have access to good accommodation. They were restricted in terms of their finances. If there were affordable day care facilities that would help. I think we need to let them know the dangers that they are exposing their children to, the dangers of abuse. My brother was placed in a previous foster home where I believe he was put in a cellar where rats bit his toes and they had to remove him. There is the danger of the natural parents losing their children for good. In Nigeria, they do it within the extended family so there is not an issue about where the child is and they know that at a certain time the child is handed back. They need to know that they can not transfer what happens in their culture to a very different culture. It is about what is best for the child. If you had asked me when I was in the foster home whether I wanted to go back to my natural parents, the answer would have been a clear no. But my best interests may well have been to go with my parents to live with them in London and then go to Nigeria.

Looking back, my experience as a private foster child must have affected me. I had a strong Christian background from my foster mother. I am still a practising Christian and I go to an international Christian centre and this is important to me. I have had a lot of changes, to my foster mother, then back to my parents, then on to Nigeria. The tendency is to think that I'd be a muddled-up person. But because I was quite fortunate in my foster home and, although I have had to go through pain, there have been things like being able to maintain contact with my foster mother and to live with her again that has balanced out the pain.

I believe it has made me a better social worker because I have gone through the experience of separation and loss myself. So when I am relating with young people, I can empathise with them.

I have been back to visit Nigeria twice so I keep in touch. I still see it as my country because that was where my parents are from. I don't know whether I could go and live there.

Margaret McMinn

Margaret McMinn was placed in a private foster home as a baby and remained there until she was 15. She later married and had children of her own.

I was born illegitimate and my mother was an Irish catholic and my father was protestant. My mother tried to keep me but had to ask other people to take care of me. At ten months, she handed me over to my father. By this time he was married (to someone else) and his wife didn't want the baby. Her mother, his mother-in-law, said she would take me in to give the marriage a chance. They owned a big farm in an isolated part.

When they got me my hair was apparently covered in nits and my earliest recollection is of her introducing me to people as the girl she took in with nits. I used to say to myself, 'Why can't you just tell them I'm yours? Why do you do this?' My other early memory is going to school on the first day. There was two miles to go and there were tinkers camped by the road and I was terrified and turned back. But I had to go alone.

If I did anything that was a nuisance, I was told that my mother was a guttersnipe. I didn't understand the word guttersnipe but I knew it was bad. I knew there was something awful about me. If I did do something wrong I was leathered with the tube from the milking machine. That did not really scare me. The terrible awfulness was that after I was leathered, I was put up in the attic bed where I slept and I was told my case was being packed and I was going to the father who did not want me. I never showed them me crying. I learnt very young not to show emotion. I wouldn't show fear.

I was well fed and I had animals. But I was lonely. Sometimes I could hear the waves coming in from the shore and I would say, 'Where will I be tomorrow night?' They had a daughter who was 13 years older than me. The 'mother' who brought me up was very much for this daughter but the 'father' did care for me but he had to be very careful that he didn't show this concern when his wife was there. He had a heart but his wife wore the trousers. I must say that, years later, when we were grown up, the daughter was very good to me.

They kept saying to me that I was different blood than their daughter was. That played havoc with me. I felt like a mongrel. They continually told me that when I was 15, I'd be sent back to my home town and I lived in dread of reaching 15. It was painful that I was not a part of this family. I must have been a nuisance to them but I was such a frightened child that I can not recall getting up to anything that was serious. If I was off school I had to work from morning to night. I even milked the cows and thinned the turnips.

I passed the exams and went to the grammar school. I made friends there, they knew I wasn't their daughter and they never mentioned it. But I didn't get on. I could not concentrate, I was obsessed with getting to 15 and being put away. The bus lifted us at seven in the morning and I wanted it to crash so I would not have to go away.

The thing that angers me most is that the school didn't question what was happening to me. Nobody wanted to put their nose in and ask anything. There were no social workers. I used their surname but nothing was signed on paper. There were people who knew about me and they used to give me money because they felt sorry for me.

I never knew who my mum was. When they said she was a guttersnipe, I used to picture her lying in the gutter drunk. The words that people say, they don't know the effect they have on children. When you are young, your mind can't get hold of it. As you get on a bit, you fear that this terrible dirt is in me. That is still with me and I now clean things unnecessarily because I fear that things will get dirty. I have to see that things are straight, I can't leave it. I used to think that if I scrubbed myself clean, my 'mother' would love me.

I saw my dad a couple of times. He was conveyed to me as a very angry and bad-tempered person. He never really had anything to do with me. He was scared to speak to me as well.

When I was 15, I went back. My bank book was emptied before I left home. I came to stay with my father and his wife but she didn't want me. I knew I had to work and get digs. I got a job in a factory where you could make money. I came home to a bed, a chair and a wardrobe. I lived in fear that I'd be paid off or that the factory would close down. I had been brought up sheltered: the only thing that I ever went to was a celeildh. I got involved with the wrong people. I had a terrible temper I was getting tense because some were being put on short-time, and I walked out. I got a job on the buses, you could work double shift and get really good money.

Then I met this feller. He wasn't good for me, he was into crime. My own father was scared of him. He was somebody who could protect me. The outcome was that I fell pregnant. He wanted me to marry him in a catholic church. For some reason, I did not want to become a catholic. Perhaps it was because a catholic mother had given me away and here I was about to go down the same road as her. I went into a Church of Scotland mother and baby home. I had a wee girl. The baby had to go into care. I was transferred to hospital. I wanted to die.

I went to find my own mother. But she didn't want to tell her husband about me. However she said that she would take my baby on condition that she be brought up as a catholic. I had nothing and I agreed. One day, I went to my mother's and I could hear my girl crying but she wasn't in. Later my child was killed in the road when she was two. There was something about my mother I didn't trust. You somehow live on. My daughter is buried in the graveyard near here. I've never been to visit because I believe she is now home so I don't see her as in a cold grave.

My husband-to-be used to come to the factory to meet me every night. I didn't want to get married. Love to me was a horrible thing. It was some two years later that I got married. It was a different love than that I'd had for my first man: that had been reckless, he had badness but he wasn't bad to me. We did get married when I was 22.

I had three boys, two were born with clubbed feet. I believed there was a curse on me. I tried to hide their feet from other people. The night one was born, I sat bolt upright in bed and said, 'Don't tell me there's a God in this world because if there is I hate him.' I was sterilised.

At that time, a bus used to go through the scheme from the Baptist church for the children. One man, Don, came to the door and asked if he could take the children to the Sunday School. I said yes but he wasn't taking me and that he shouldn't even mention that name God to me.

Then I found I had cancer. The doctor put me on the priority waiting list and in the meantime gave me valium. I was taken into the hospital very quickly. Another woman went in with me as an emergency and that night she disintegrated. I thought, 'Why have I lived and she die for she was a very quiet woman?' That night, the hard shell began to break.

Don started to take me to meetings and I began to hear more and more about this being born again and I started to thirst for it. I was thinking it's because I'm illegitimate that I can't get into God's Kingdom. The understanding came in and that was it. I had to see that He died, not for the world, for me.

I hope your book will show that wee children have emotions and that these emotions have to be allowed to come up. It affects me now. If someone in the church says something, I can feel so rejected. I see a lot of mistakes in the way I've brought up my children. With my eldest, I would only cuddle him when nobody was about. I was following my childhood through again. I look at my daughter-in-laws and how they are with their children, they are much more emotional. I don't think I am emotional with my husband. It is only since coming to the Lord that I have let my emotions out.

It is the security you have in love as a child that keeps you on in life. Now I've found that security of love in Christ. It has given me the opportunity to go back to college. I was in hotel work and I went to college, I was over 40, to study cleaning sciences and business studies. I came out joint top. But then I got stressed out at the job and I went to a psychologist and a psychiatrist. They considered going back into my childhood but the senior said no because it could open it up and have nothing to replace it.

I couldn't live through it again. It did build strengths in me. I can endure. I've had to be tough. But I've made it.

71

Rena Rogers

Rena is now 15 and has been with her private foster mother, Ms Clare Bryan, for five years.

When I was young I lived with my mum and dad and two sisters. My dad started to get drunk a lot and come in at all hours. As I got older, I began to look after my sisters myself when my mum went out with my dad. Then my dad passed away. My mum couldn't cope with us. I went to quite a few places. I went to a children's home then came back. Then my mum gave us to our grandmother. My sisters were put in a foster home and then adoption. I used to play with Clare's little nieces and I got to know Clare. I started coming round her home and sometimes when my grandmother used to leave me, Clare would take me at night. I went to a foster home which I did not like. I asked if I could live with Clare and my social worker allowed it. So I came here.

Clare looks after me. She treats me well. She brings me up well. When I was living with my mum, I didn't go to school much. Clare gets me to go. She buys me things, buys me clothes. I can talk with her. I like going to the church. We sing and learn about the bible and we hear about paradise and things like that. I go out with Clare and we sell charity tickets. I also go to the army cadets on Saturday nights. I go to a dancing and drama group.

I don't see my mum much now. It's supposed to be every fortnight. I don't miss her much but I miss my sisters, they are six and seven now. I get to see them twice a year. I go up and have a holiday with them.

I've explained to my friends at school that I live with Clare and they understand. I see myself staying here. I'd like to get qualified in computers and be a secretary. I'd like to get a car one day.

The social worker is helpful in some ways. He asks me whether I like it here and do I get enough time to see my sisters? But they have a different social worker.

Mary Tapper

Mary Tapper spent much of her childhood in a private foster home. She is a qualified nurse, is married and has children.

I was brought up by my family in Sierra Leone. My father, although illiterate, had a peanut plantation and provided very well for the family. One day, aged seven, I found myself in a teacher's house and a totally strange environment. My parents probably thought they were doing the best for me by giving me to a teacher. My mum was in the same town but on the other side of it. The teacher

72

took me to look after her own children, aged six and four. She was very abusive physically and hit me with rods, I still have nightmares over that, and she broke one of my fingers.

A couple of years or so later, she brought us all to England. I think I got a glimpse of my mum as the ship was leaving. From a wonderful sunny place we arrived at Liverpool where it was grey and horrible. We were in London for a few months then one day we were on a train and finished up in Kent. I was ten. My brother and sister, as I call them, also came to be put in a foster home.

When we arrived, the private foster mother was not there and we were taken in by the private foster father. We were put to bed then I woke up. By this time, the foster mother came in and said she didn't want any black kids in her house. Being the eldest I was more sensitive about what was going on. I was worried because we were not wanted. I wondered, 'Where is our mum, as I called the teacher?' She never came to see us, that was the awful thing. She had never discussed about what was happening to us. She never wrote.

The next morning we were verbally abused again. The foster mother said she didn't want any black faces in the house. I can remember thinking if only I could just shrink or disappear. I was worried about the younger ones. I felt very shocked about the whole transaction, finding myself in another place and this time in a different culture with white foster parents. It obviously damaged me.

A few weeks later, my foster father started to sexually abuse me. I was 11. You get yourself into a kind of mood where it's not you it's happening to. I remember thinking that if he was doing it to me then he's not going to do it with the younger ones. But he was abusing them as well. I think the foster mother knew it was going on but she buried her head in the sand. The foster father is now dead. Recently I did confront her with it and she said she was scared of the man.

My sister buried herself in academic things. She was reading all the time. My brother adopted being Simple Simon. A couple of years after we went there, my mum, the teacher, sent another child, the youngest, to join us. She has a lot of psychological problems now.

I went to the primary school for half a year and then to senior school. It was difficult at school at first because, although we spoke English, it was Creole, broken English and French. They thought I was very simple because I did not have any language. They did not realise I was struggling with it. I was put in a special needs class. I did not do well academically but I had been a bright child at school in Africa. With all the trauma, I went into a shell. I knew what was going on but I could not put it on to paper. I could not talk to any teachers about what was going on at home.

We made good friends but I did not want to get involved with them because I didn't want them to get the same treatment. I would go and see them but I would not invite them back as I wanted to protect them. They wanted to come to my home for a change but I didn't want them to come.

The social services did find out we were there. This was only because the money had run out from my parents. But never once did we get to talk to the social worker without our foster parents there. Before he came, we were told you had better not say anything or you will go back to Africa. It was the time of the Biafran war with terrible pictures of children on TV. So, of course, I was scared. In fact, we were sort of ignored while my foster father conversed with the social worker. At no time did the social worker even try to talk to us individually. I wanted so badly to tell what was happening but I never got the opportunity to do so. Even now it is very difficult because the nightmare still lives on. I carry the guilt of thinking that if I had behaved myself this would not have happened.

My foster mother is naturally a kind person but she doesn't know how to show it. At birthdays and Christmas, they always bought gifts but there was never affection. It is only now that I understand.

I left home aged 17. By this time I had completely lost contact with my mum, the teacher. I went to a nurses' home. I was scared of the world so I lived-in. I had to pass the entrance exam to a hospital. It was without the support of anybody. I had to prove I could do it.

After I qualified as a nurse, I decided I would go to Jamaica because I was involved with a Jamaican person. The relationship broke up but I still wanted to go there to nurse. By this time I had a daughter. I could not cope with all the oppression and poverty around me. After six months, I went to Chicago and stayed with people I'd met in Jamaica. By this time my daughter was two. I worked as a day care assistant and then as an *au pair* looking after two children. After a year I got married but really I think it was only to get a dad for my daughter. I got pregnant soon after and my son was born. He was diagnosed as autistic.

My partner became a violent alcoholic. Meanwhile I had found my faith as a Jehovah's Witness and I got great support from the congregation. It was my stability. In the end I managed to get to England.

My foster mother put us up. I had been in America for ten years and was not working. My son was ten, my daughter 16. My son was very difficult and was excluded from school but social services were not helpful. They called a meeting and a friend told me, 'Leave him here.' My childhood came back, I thought 'Am I doing the same thing?' They did take him and I was scared that I was going to lose him. He went to a special unit.

After a couple of years I met my husband and we married in 1995. We discovered that my daughter has Asbergers Syndrome, a mild form of autism. She is now 18 and works in the same nursing home as me, looking after the elderly.

I found out a few years ago that the people I was trying to protect, my siblings, were also being abused. I couldn't protect them. Even now it's a nightmare which I still have to live. I don't want any other child to experience what we experienced as children.

Being fostered had a profound effect on me. It made me not trust. I lost confidence in my own judgement. Even when I know what I am doing is right, I am never 100 per cent sure. I have been like a parent all my life, never a child. I lost that when I left my natural parents. It happened in both the lands where I spent my formative years. I did have a loving family until I was seven. I drew my strength from that. We were close and tactile. I miss that.

I still see my brother and sisters, as I call them, who were in the foster home with me. He is 42 and works in the post office. One sister is a finance manager and the youngest has a degree and is doing teacher training. None of them have criminal records or anything like that. We were frightened into being submissive.

There should be liaison between the schools and social services. If a new child comes to a school and the teacher sees it as a private fostering, they should tell the social services. The social worker who visited us should have picked up that something was completely wrong. He didn't really care. We did have a lot in the foster home like music instruments and the social worker would play the clarinet. He was more the foster parents' friend than ours. He should have been more aware of the body language of children. I'd like to be a social worker because I could pick up the signs in children.

I have lost my culture. I am neither African nor western. I am more western and I would not know how to be a full African. I have a friend from Sierra Leone but our ways of thinking are different. My dream is to go to Sierra Leone. Even if my parents are not alive, I just want to touch that soil.

Roland Webb

Roland Webb was a private foster child for 16 years in the same foster home as Sylvia Ackfield. After a career in the police force, he took early retirement.

I was born in Croydon in 1950. I have now seen the place where I was born. It was a kind of private nursing home. I guess it was a place where people had a child born out of wedlock and one party had money.

My mother had married in 1941. I have actually spoken with her ex-husband. It was a war-time arrangement. He went off to fight the war, she went to London and they parted. My father's name was Steele. He was very high in the civil service. My name went down as Webb. I started researching my background after I divorced in 1985 when I wanted to find out about myself. I went to Dulwich where my mother had lived and then to the place in Sydenham where I visited her two or three times. I found out that my mother had died two years before, of cancer. It upset me because it had taken me all those years to get to terms with wanting to make a kind of peace. I would never have viewed her as a parent. She was very selfish. But I would like to have exchanged Christmas cards, but it would never have been a close relationship because I was in a foster home from the age of one to 17. Mary was my mother's best friend. She told me that my mother was a workaholic. She said that my mother was in a convalescent home suffering from cancer: she looked out at the beach and turned to Mary and said, 'These mothers with sons'. Mary says that she wished that she had tried to get hold of me. I feel she did not do anything about it even when she was dying. I am not concerned about not being left anything in the will: what I did not have in life, I would not want in death.

I don't know what happened to me in the first year. I know I went to the foster home in 1952. I went back to the child care officer who used to visit me and one of the other foster children. She told me I had a quick temper. Once, I was two or three, I was given a train set by my mother and father and I threw it at my foster mother. I said that showed I was not going to be bought off. I always resented presents from that source at Christmas because I never saw them at Christmas.

There was never any doubt that we were foster children because the numbers varied. There were long term ones like me but also short term who came for a few days. There wasn't a male figure in the house, just a foster mother. She was very Victorian, she read the bible. She was very reliable, very overprotective. She had local authority children as well as private ones. She would get a phone call on a Friday evening, 'Can you take so and so?' We used to dread it. Over the years, there were six to eight long term children. I met up with one who was the first foster child. Auntie, as we called our foster mother, wanted to adopt her.

In the foster home, there wasn't any closeness or affection. If you fell down, you were told to shut up, not 'come here'. It was a very cold place, no central heating. I used to dread the winters. Food we grew ourselves in the large garden. There were ducks, chickens and pigs. When I first went, there was one other boy but I was the only bloke for the last eight to ten years so I did much of the work.

Auntie was very strict and honest. We were not allowed to mix with people in the village. Once we came in from school, that was it which meant that you became isolated which affects your social ability. We always went to church because we formed the church choir. As I got older, I started to do jobs around the village, cut the grass, keep the gardens, which meant I could earn some money. One of my proudest things was to save up for a school blazer because I went to Midhurst Grammar School. My real mother said she couldn't afford it. Auntie was not a talker. She had very strict views on the role of women. She would have been very proud of Margaret Thatcher. Unfortunately she died in 1971. She was never a person who spoke about how she felt. She never spoke about her family in the village, never showed emotion. She wasn't a person to get close to. We had a TV when I was about 13. She dictated when we used it; the news, Peter Scott, David Attenborough and horse jumping. We were told to read. It was normal for the time. We were not encouraged to play amongst ourselves. At one time there were about 15 of us, we all had our own garden, we didn't have shouting, screaming, laughter, the normal things with kids. She did the best that she knew. The good thing was that I was in one place for my childhood. It wasn't maybe a happy place but it was one place. We didn't have any kind of abuse. We were not hit or beaten. Once she was painting the scullery, I was in my early teens, and I asked her, 'Why am I here? What am I doing here?' It was clearly the wrong question for the brush came out and whack. She didn't mean to hit me in that way but that was her reaction. One of the sad things was that no one was encouraged to ask.

When I saw the child care officer, in 1987, she told me that when I was about ten, she came to see auntie. Normally she came by appointment and we had to be on our best behaviour. She was concerned about our development and that we were not mixing with people. My child care officer said that auntie assured her that our parents came down every other week and took us out. It was a complete lie and I was quite shocked about that.

There were four to five social workers who called over the time I was there. As the main one later told me, their only responsibility was to see that we were fed and watered. They had no control over the educational side. She came about every two months. She only saw me in the presence of my aunt and she told me what to say. You could not have a heart-to-heart with auntie or anybody. But I would not be put down. Some of the other children were like mice. There was always something inside me that said I was not going to be trodden on.

My parents always paid on time. Auntie knew the cheque would come. My parents lived together until I was about ten. They used to come down every month or every other month by train or bus for an afternoon. I had to go and meet them and was supposed to be affectionate which I didn't want to be. Then, when I was about ten, I was told that I would not see him any more. I wasn't given much explanation and I couldn't ask auntie anything. They lived together in a very nice house in Dulwich. She started coming on her own and appeared in a car and having a very different kind of life style. I thought, 'And I am having to find a school uniform'. My father had stuck by her for some time. He was about 30 years older than her. He died when he was 94, she died when she was 61–62, within a year of each other

She kept coming every month or so. She would then come with some other man who I later found out was married. When I was about 14, I went to see her in London. She met me at Waterloo and we went to her place. There was a glass door and great big Chinese vases, I'd never seen anything like it. Then she prepared a meal, peppers which I had never seen. Then I helped with the washing up. We only had hot water once a week from one of those grey boilers with smoke everywhere. I couldn't understand here why there was no smoke, no fire, I didn't know about immersion heaters. I got up in the morning and I thought I'd make a cup of tea for her. I went in the room and she was in bed with this other man. I'd led a very sheltered childhood. I packed my bags and left the house and made my way home. I only saw her once after that. We spoke on the phone when I started work. It should not have been like that. I was their only son and it would have been lovely if, later, they had seen me pass out at the police parade. It was almost more their loss than mine.

I studied the violin. I didn't want to but I passed five exams. When I was 11 or 12, I did get extra tuition in algebra and English in the evening. I don't know who paid for it. At school you were always different, you dressed differently. The other children were not hostile but you were not allowed to mix with them after school, go to youth clubs or anything like that. You didn't have the pocket money, you didn't have the nice things which other kids had. You were not picked on at school but you were different because you didn't have a mother or father. The teachers were very understanding. At grammar school, when I was playing up, I think they turned a blind eye to some of the things I was doing such as booking in the morning then going out. We had to do homework. I might not have enjoyed it but I got O levels, the only one from our home. I think there was an expectation that I came from a good background from the point of view that my father had a very high job in the civil service and my mother was an accountant.

I started on A levels but I left. I felt that if I had stayed there I was being prepared to work on a farm. From the age of 13–14, I felt there was more to me than that. I decided I was going to leave the foster home. The only way I could leave was by being kicked out and so I became very aggressive and argumentative. There were only three of us in the home by this time. I was the man about the house but not the man. I didn't have any contact with my father, little with my mother. I had never had a father's influence. I had to get out. From the age of 15, I used to go to the local youth club. We had to be in bed at 9pm and by this time I had a bedroom of my own and used to climb out and get on my push bike to the youth club. Then I went to the pubs and had a pint of mild and got back at 11–12. By this time I was answering auntie back so there was a very unhappy atmosphere. I engineered a final flare-up which ended in auntie saying, 'I want you out of here by the end of the week'. It was extremely cruel of me but I thought it was the only way I'd ever get out. I don't think she really meant it.

I went to the local careers place and they fixed me up with an interview with a hotel which I got as a trainee waiter. It gave me a roof over my head, some food and a start in life. I was 17. I always kept in touch with auntie after that. The last time I spoke to my mother, I was in the first hotel. She phoned me up and wanted to know how much I was earning as it affected her tax code. She'd given me a cheque for my birthday which I had never cashed. I'd passed my driving test and wanted to buy a new car and needed £50 for a deposit. I'd never asked her for anything in my life. She said no. That was the last time I ever spoke to her. She never came to see me, never asked how I got on.

I did very well in the hotel business. I was taken on to the hotel chain's official management programme, became assistant manager of a big hotel and then went to the head office in London. I was really a workaholic and drank too much because I was not having days off.

After London, I decided to join the police. I was 20. After two years, I met the woman who was to be my wife. She did not like what I was doing so I went to work for Norwich Union. I always yearned to go back in the police and after two years I went back in Staffordshire. I was there five years, passed the sergeant and inspector exams but the rule was I could not get promotion for ten years. I then saw an advertisement for Thames Valley police which was where I had worked before so I got it. I did a degree through the Open University. Later I lost confidence. Things were not right in the marriage. When we were divorced it was as amicable as any divorce could be. No one else was involved. I was working long hours. I used to have migraines. I was involved in all the high profile events in Thames Valley. I left the police early in 1998. There was a restructuring and I went on early retirement. It was an economic decision but targeted at persons. It angered me because I was very well qualified. I turned down three times the offer to join the Lodge and that made life much harder. I had my own moral high ground. Other people were getting jobs and positions without interviews. It angered me because I was very well qualified.

Since leaving the police, I've had three jobs, as a charity mobile information officer, a building society manager and emergency services manager with the WRVS.

I'd never really looked at my personal life. There is a woman at the hospital, in charge of the voluntary services. She showed me a clipping about a book on self-counselling. I got it. It wasn't bedtime reading but it was really helpful. It was mainly case studies which showed how people repeated behaviour and the message was that I'd got to break the cycle I was in. I was getting into relationships where unhappy people were treating me like their ex. I could see myself in some of the case studies. With my ex-wife, I would not say how I was feeling. I would then sulk for about three days and would not talk. Life is better now. This is how things should have been years ago. I am now in a job which I enjoy. It's not a seven days a week job and I've time for other things. I don't want to hide myself in work because that is what my parents did. I'm in a pathway which I've never really taken before.

Regarding my fostering experience, I look first at the positive. I've had to make choices and decisions about my life. Decisions which other people don't know how to do. I'm very sensitive about people and am able to assess them. I seem to know more about people without them telling me. I can tell when people are lying. It has made me sensitive and caring about people but not soft. The strength of my upbringing has helped me cope with parents who did not do what I wanted them to do. I'm proud of that.

Some of my life has been a psychological hell. The negative side is that I don't really feel a part. As you get older that gets worse. I must be careful as I get older of falling into wrong relationships. We've all got to try and sort things out for ourselves. It's not having things explained to me, not understanding why. They were both intelligent people yet they chose, for some reason unknown to me, not to do it. That was very cruel. It is a shame for them as well because I wouldn't have hated them: I don't actually hate them now, I feel very sad.

I would like to have had the option of being adopted. I don't mean by auntie. I mean by a mother and father. But my real mother would not let that happen. I think children should always know why they are there, have it explained to them and that should be a continual process. It has to grow inside you so that you understand. Parents must realise what an impact it has on children. They can shut their children out and that's what happened with me.

Chapter 7: The Private Foster Carers

Mrs Marlene Box

Mrs Marlene Box is married with four children. Her own mother was a child minder.

My daughter, who was 15 at the time, came home with a friend, Lorna, who'd been chucked out and had nowhere to live, could she stay with us? We were converting the attic into a bedroom and the two girls could sleep there, so what was one more mouth to feed?

She came with a lot of problems. She was a self-harmer and anorexic. Her mother had the mental age of about a ten year old. There was something drastically wrong with her. She was living with a partner who was epileptic. Her father had re-married and was living with his second wife and had a child of about five. Lorna was brought up mainly by her gran and by her mum until they could not cope. Then she went to live with her dad for 15 months. The stepmother couldn't get on with her, they were nervous about their own child. She didn't talk and they couldn't understand the eating problems.

When she came here, I informed her dad. He said that he didn't care if she was living in a cardboard box in the street. He brought all her things round and dumped them out on the drive. After she came, she had hardly any contact with her mum and dad. She hated her mum. In some ways her mum was lovely but she wasn't all the ticket. When she did come to see Lorna, she (Lorna) didn't want to know, she was embarrassed by her and her mum used to cry when she left. A little while before she left here, she let on that her mum and step-dad used to go down to the pub and take her with them and they'd get drunk and she'd have to sit there. Apparently, when she was about seven, one night Lorna didn't want to go and they left her in the house on her own. They came back with some friends and one of the men started messing with Lorna. I took her to the police about this but nothing came of it. The police videoed her but said it was too long ago. I wondered if this was her problem. I told the social worker about it but they did nothing.

She came about two years ago and I had her for 13 months. She was fine at first, very quiet. I could understand her eating problems because I've got them. I knew where she was coming from and I knew exactly what games she was playing. She had a communication problem. Occasionally she'd come over and I'd look at her and say, 'Do you want a cuddle?' And she'd look at me, come over, sob her heart out and cuddle. She was treated like part of the family. The kids adored her and she was great with them. We had problems with her at school, she was always skiving, and in the end she had a home tutor: it was just twice a week for one hour which wasn't very good. Although she was quiet, she would do anything for attention. She was giggly and flirty.

The social services were absolutely useless. They did speak to Lorna on her own but she could not communicate with them very well. The one person she could communicate with was me. It wasn't brilliant but I used to get little bits out. They arranged for her to go to a psychiatrist and I used to take her. It was no help. I went to all the foster meetings because they told me we could foster her officially. I thought it would help her mentally if she knew where she stood and show that I did care and understand her problems. Then on New Years Eve, they phoned to inform us that her dad didn't want her to be fostered and was arranging for her to live with his 73 year old grandmother, which never happened.

So I was never paid properly. Her mother kept the child benefit book for months. I spent £360 on clothes for her because she had nothing. I got in contact with the Child Support Agency and, at one point, the father owed us over £1,000, then it was reduced to £900, then £600 and then they wrote to say he owed us £264.

In the end Lorna ran away. I'd let another bloke stay here. He was 21, a manic-depressive, didn't have a job. My own daughter moved out and went and stayed with my mum. We were going on holiday for two weeks and took them with us. It was a lovely holiday, everything the kids had, they had. Basically they were having what they missed out on in their own childhood. We got back on the Tuesday. I was at work, I work 40 hours a week in a shop to keep everybody, when I got a phone call to say no one had been to pick up my son from his playgroup. The two of them had gone off together. I got in contact with the police. Nothing could be done. I phoned the school and the social services. I heard that the social services in another place had taken over. They may still be together, they can only harm each other.

Since she left, she hasn't written. I haven't seen her parents. I really did work hard with her. I feel very bitter. She was very disturbed. My kids were devastated when she left. They adored her and couldn't understand why. I'll never forgive them for that.

Ms Clare Bryan

Clare Bryan experienced a deprived childhood with many traumas. Perhaps these experiences made her willing to take in a private foster child.

I was brought up in a broken family. My brother went into care. My dad used to abuse me violently. I left home at 13 and lived on the streets. I got into drugs and into wrong things. I've had a hard life. I've been there, I know what it is like for children who've got nobody.

I struggled out of it. Worked as a hairdresser and married an Asian guy, a Moslem. I knew Rena. She lived up the road from me and a few times I'd come in late at night and she'd still be out on the streets. Rena used to play with my sister's kids and I got to know her. I wanted a child of my own and was trying to get pregnant but I did not go after Rena. She had gone to live with her grandmother then one day social services knocked on my door and said that Rena had been asking for me and could she live with me. I explained that I wasn't a relative or a friend of the family. I took her in, she was ten and she is going on 15 now. She came not long before Christmas. Being married to an Asian, I hadn't celebrated it. So I had to go out and buy a Christmas tree and presents. She had nothing when she came, nothing. I've given her a life.

My husband didn't like me having Rena. There were problems in the marriage and it broke down. But by this time I was pregnant. I lost the child, perhaps because of the stress of my marriage breakdown. I took Rena in but she wasn't a baby. Really she helped me pull through. I had to keep going. Sometimes when I'm on my own, I sit and cry and think about my husband. Then I think of what I went through on the streets. She kept me going because I knew I had to get up each day and get her ready for school. And after school there had to be a meal ready. I had to change my whole life from freedom to revolving around a child. It took me a couple of years to adapt to that.

Rena is a good kid but she has had a lot of problems. Her father is dead and she had nightmares. Lately she has opened up and she can talk about things which have happened in her past, like the times she lived away. I've had no help from social services over these things. I've done it all off my own bat. So I've done courses in counselling and they've helped me understand her. It is hard. Sometimes she drives me mad with her behaviour. I'm only 26 and it is more like having a younger sister yet I've got to be a mother first to her and I do feel she is a part of me. So I've had to put down rules but too often I give in to her.

Before she came to me, she never went to school. Since she's been with me she has been going every day and her reports say she is doing well, although there are friends who distract her. I want her to do well at GCSEs and when she is 16 she can decide what to do. I never went to school. I haven't got one exam. I'm having to do it now. I don't want her to end up like me. I study with her and I get a private tutor for her because she is a bit low in her class. I don't pay this tutor because she is a friend of mine from the church. I go to Jehovah's Witnesses. They come to the house and we study the bible together. Rena goes to the church on Sunday. I'm not a Jehovah's Witness but it's good to learn what's in the bible. Rena goes and does a youth book which is about education, about parents, about alcohol.

Rena is good at cleaning, she can cook now. When she gets her own accommodation, when she is older, she'll be able to support herself. No matter what she has been through, I want her to know that she has pulled through. Rena is good about money. They want named clothes. It's £60 for trainers. So I'll buy her a pair and say, 'Make these last until your birthday or Christmas' and she does. She's never had it before so when she gets something good she will look after it.

There is a difficulty for Rena now that she goes to see her sisters who are younger than her and are a long way away. Rena doesn't know what to say. They are asking, 'Why are we here in a foster home and you there?' Her mum and dad used to go out drinking and Rena used to look after her sisters a lot. Now they are asking her for photos of dad. But Rena's dad isn't their dad and they don't know. It isn't fair to tell them that Rena's dad has passed away. Somehow they need to know but Rena doesn't want to tell them.

Her mum is a drinker and it is probably good that she doesn't come very often. But Rena should have contact. When she comes here, she sees Rena with a life and you can see tears in her eyes. She regrets giving her up but she did what was best for her. I don't want her to think I am trying to take her place. Your mum's your mum, you can never replace her. At one time, Rena didn't want to know her but I said you've got to think why your mum did it and she did it to give you a good life.

Her mum has never paid me anything. For three and a half years, I've done it on my own. When I was on Income Support, I got paid for her. Now I get child benefit. I had no help from the social services. Then I told them, 'You've got to help me or I can't continue doing this'. They had a few meetings and it was agreed that they would give me some financial help and that Rena could stay until she was 18. I think they might take me on officially. The social worker only comes about once a month because they know she is all right. He takes Rena out or they go up to the bedroom to have a talk. He'll ask her how she is getting on. If I feel down and she is playing me up, he'll sit down and we'll try and work round it. So he's pretty good. It's just that I don't think he knows what to do.

For three and a half years, the social services was not useful. I think they thought I was taking Rena in for the money but I had no money from anybody. I've proved them wrong. I saw a needy child that was starving and needed help. If you saw a photo of her then, she looked so ill, withdrawn and thin. Now she's put on weight and she's got colour in her face. If she wasn't with me she'd be in care and they'd have to pay. I told the social worker that and he wasn't too happy. They have paid for Rena to visit her sisters. If there is a meeting with social services, I'll keep Rena off school so that she's there. I don't think it is right that we should sit there and discuss things that she doesn't know.

She's a companion for me. Sometimes I feel I'd no love in my life after my marriage broke down. She keeps me going every day. If I lived on my own I don't think I'd be so esteemed as I am now. To see a child who had nothing, to see what she is like now, her education, clubs, certificates, she is making something of her life—to see that she's done well makes me proud. I can see that she can do something with her life and I don't want her to throw it away. I thank God for her. God must have brought us together.

Mr and Mrs Cahalin

Mr and Mrs Cahalin have fostered for a local authority as well as taking private foster children. In all they have cared for 11 private foster children.

Mr: We came from Warwickshire that's where we fostered. I worked as an aerospace engineer. After 20 years I got made redundant and the only job I could get was here in this city. So we moved. Now my spine has crumbled, through work and playing rugby.

Mrs. My mum was an unofficial child minder. I left school at 16 and went to be a nanny, came back and got married and did child minding. Then we started fostering with the local authority. We did that for a few years and then went into private fostering. I had this thing about little children. I can't leave them alone. I'd rather play with little children than do anything.

Mr: Once we had six, all from the one family, from the local authority. Then it went through a stage with the local authority when we stopped getting little ones and were getting older ones. My wife was still getting *Nursery World* which was full of adverts for private foster kids. We started with one phone call and the rest followed by word of mouth. Often the parents didn't know us from Adam. But they knew others who said we were good foster parents and they'd come with a baby and be in and out in an hour.

Mrs: 10 o'clock on a Sunday morning, a phone call from a couple, I had to ask them to repeat themselves three times as their English was not that good. But you pick up words like, 'I am Nigerian', 'I am a friend of . . .' They were here by 12 o'clock and gone by 12.30. The only annoying thing was when they spoke to each other in their own language.

Mr: One little lad we had for seven to eight months then his mum and dad took him and emigrated to Canada. We had a phone call from his mum to say he couldn't stand the extremes of weather out there and would we have him. We went to Gatwick to meet the mother and child, brought them back home for a barbecue and then she went back to Canada. We had him until he was four.

Mrs: At one time we had four private foster children, three local authority children and our own three sons. There was only one who couldn't settle. For eight days he just sobbed and cried. He wanted his mum and I wasn't his mum. Otherwise all settled in because they were babies, the youngest was six weeks when he came, the oldest two and a half. The very young one came from a couple who were in digs in London while she was pregnant. A woman on their landing had her baby knifed while she was robbed so they just wanted to get out of it as soon as possible and so I took the baby at six weeks. They usually stay until they are five.

I asked one of the mums why they fostered out their children. She said that the men wouldn't marry the women until they knew they could have children. By this time they were working, so what do you do with your child? They are in London and may have to be at work by 8 o'clock so they've got to be up at 6. You leave work at 5 and then you've got to travel to pick up your child from a minder. It's a hell of a long day and you don't see anything of your child. So it's best to foster. A lot went to college. Most of the women were at college and worked part-time to support themselves.

Mr: Most of the parents settled in Britain. They arrive in this country, foster their children out and then start on their careers.

Mrs: We've had very few problems with the children. They've all thrived. I only had one accident. One was 'dancing' and hit the door, just over his eye. The hospital would not treat him until they'd phoned his mother, even though I'd already got her written consent to any treatment. And one boy was really angry. Always bad tempered. He wasn't miserable but he was always angry. All the others at the same age, two to three, were really lovely. One child had sickle cell anaemia. I didn't know anything about it but I soon learnt. Antibiotics every day, fruit all the while. And they do tend to fall asleep at odd times. We have to put special oil on their hair. There were no problems with eating. The parents were not upset about them having meat and three veg.

Mr: We couldn't cope with the child with sickle cell. We had to lie to the mother to get her to take her back.

Mrs: It was disrupting everything. If she fell asleep then you couldn't disturb her until she woke and she could sleep for three hours. If you've got children waiting at the school gates it's not on. She needed one to one care. One day I phoned the mother and put on a Welsh accent and told her that the foster mother was ill and would she come and get the child. The mother asked 'the Welsh woman' if she would take her.

Mr: One little boy was nearly three and not speaking and we spent hours trying to get him to speak. Most of the parents have been brilliant. There was one who said she was going to pick the baby up for Christmas. Came the day she was supposed to come: no. We tried the phone number she had left us and nobody knew her. So we phoned the local police. Then on Boxing Day, the father came to pick him up and we never did find out what happened to the mum. Others have been brilliant. One of the mothers was training to be a pharmacist. She'd been fostered when she was a child so it was the norm to find foster parents for her own child. She became a good friend. The ones who went to Canada used to ring every month. Then the mum would come over and stay with us for 2–3 days and then go back to see relatives in London, then back to us for a few days.

Mrs: The parents visit about once every 4–6 months. But often they phone regularly and I try to get the kids to giggle over the phone. We got very attached to the children. But often the parents didn't actually say when they were coming to collect their children. We had two children and the parents rang and said, 'Can we have the children for a fortnight?' I said, 'Of course, let me know when you are coming and I'll get their stuff ready'. They came unexpectedly, they took the children and we never saw them again. But another parent told me how upset one of the children was at being pulled away from us.

Payment has always been up front. I had a set rate and kept a diary about the payments. The parents kept the child benefit. We never had a problem about it. We charged £25 a week for the first baby so we didn't exactly make a profit. We used to have 70 pints of milk a week, then there was food and clothes. At one time we had a cleaner in while I played with the children.

Mr: I had a really well-paid job and we needed it. We lived in a five bedroomed detached house. People who say you go into private fostering for the money don't know what they are talking about. If you don't love kids you wouldn't do it.

Mrs: Occasionally, I'd be walking down a street and a car would pull up and a chap call out, 'nigger lover'. You get quite a lot of looks.

Mr: They never said anything while I was there. Mind you, I was an 18 stone front row forward.

Mrs: Private fostering is different from local authority because we didn't have contact with the social worker over them. We had to tell them when the children came and that was it.

Mr: They have got more responsibility now but they didn't then. Our local authority social worker was great. He had been educated in the university of life, he'd done other jobs before he was a social worker. He'd drop in and have a cup of coffee. But he was for the children who were in care. We informed them when we took private foster children but they didn't do any checks. There were places in the area where about 12–15 families had private foster children. They all came from London and advertised in *Nursery World*. But the law changed and they could not advertise. But private fostering goes on only it is underground.

Mrs: Having foster children has not hurt our own children. Our eldest is 24. He can only just remember a time, apart from now, when there were not other children around. The next is 17 and the third is 15. I think it has benefited them. They are much more tolerant: they've seen a wide aspect of life.

Mr: We have had some good times. I remember when I was on night duty and I used to come in and ask, 'how many have we got?' my wife used to reply, 'there's another one upstairs'.

Mrs: I'd love to foster again.

Pauline Hawkins

Pauline Hawkins is in her late 30s. She is close to her parents and three siblings. She has lived in the same small town most of her life.

Four years ago, I was living with Noreen's father. He is from abroad but had come to England. He'd been married there and one Christmas his former wife sent their daughter to stay with him for six weeks. She was going into the bush for a few weeks with her boyfriend. Noreen was seven and she was put on the plane all alone for an 11 hour flight. She was like a stick insect, so thin. She had dirty clothes, her hair was matted. It turned out that she had had big problems, had run away and tried to take her own life. She had had a terrible life there and been neglected and sent to every Tom, Dick and Harry. So he went to court and got a residence order so she stayed in England.

Three months later, Noreen wasn't getting on with her dad so there was friction at home. I was trying to please everybody. Noreen was arguing with her dad and, in the end, I decided to leave as it was making me ill.

Noreen wanted to come with me, she didn't want to stay with her father. She even tried to take her own life. She hadn't really known him as he had left their home country when she was two. When we met her off the plane, she had taken an instant liking to me. I'd looked after her almost full-time as her dad had been working and was hardly ever at home, he was out at the pub a lot. I gave up my job to look after her and she grew fond of me. I gave her all the time and attention that she needed and she lapped it up. I'd gone back to live with my parents. I thought it best to get the SSD involved as I didn't know how to handle the situation. They agreed she could stay with me at my parents' place for a few weeks. There was one big meeting at the SSD and then, even without consulting Noreen, they decided that she had to stay with her dad. Noreen was very distressed so they decided she should go into official foster care. She went to a place for a couple of weeks and I was allowed to see her once a week. She was in tears everyday, it was heartbreaking. She didn't want to be parted from me. So there was another meeting, her dad was there, and it was agreed that the best place for her was with me. So we went back to live with my parents. My parents' flat was too small so we had to go into a homeless hostel and luckily we were only there for two weeks and then I was allowed this flat and I got her into the local school.

It has been very traumatic and without my mum's help I wouldn't be coping. It is very difficult because Noreen doesn't want contact with either of her parents. Her dad wants to see her but at the moment he is back in his country on holiday. He wasn't very nice to her even in front of me when were living together. Nearly everyday, if she didn't do what he said he would say, 'I'm getting a plane ticket for you back to where you came from'. It was mental torture because from what she said had happened to her over there, she knew what it would be like.

She's a lovely child. Normally she's as happy as anything. The social worker was here a couple of days ago and asked her, 'Are you happy?' She said, 'Yes, I'm happy if I don't have to talk about things that upset me and make me angry'. Apart from that she's the happiest child alive. And she is doing so well at school. And that reflects back on me, it shows I'm doing my job properly. She goes to some clubs at the school. She was in a play. I went to see it all three nights so by the third night I knew almost every word. We go out at weekends. This Saturday, I am going to take her swimming. She is brainy for her years but she's also had to grow up, she's nine going on for 19. She doesn't like going to bed so we have little tantrums then. But no child wants to go to bed at night. Now and then, she'll think about the past, recently she was talking about when she was in foster care for two weeks and how hard that was for her and the next minute she was bawling her eyes out. At certain times she'll sit and talk about life with her mother and little things come out. I don't think she's old enough to discuss some of the things she's witnessed. I try to explain that to the social workers, I'm with her most of the time and I know what makes her tick. You can't learn it from a textbook.

I haven't got any security. Noreen feels secure here but it is not 100 per cent because she knows that at any time she could be removed. We have another meeting next month and that is going to bring up about me applying for a residence order to make it more secure for Noreen and for myself. At present her dad has the residence order and could take her at any time. He has told me that he would not do that because he knows it would upset her too much. But there is always that 1 in 100 chance that one day he would. Noreen says, 'He will not move me' and she is such a strong willed person that it would take a bulldozer to actually move her from here. I talk to her dad because I have to. Noreen wants no contact with him and the agreement is that he has contact via me. He should come over to find out what Noreen is doing, how she is getting on at school, then, at least, she would know that somebody cares. She doesn't like him coming.

I do get child benefit but I am on income support so I don't get a lot. Without my mum I couldn't do it. Before I had Noreen, I had a job and was all right for money. So I went from a good wage to basically nothing. I became an instant mother with a seven year old child in my care. I wasn't used to it: I'd never had any of my own. It was difficult to cope financially but I was willing to do it to make sure that Noreen was happy and safe. She is and that's my reward. I could have had a full-time job, might have been married. After everything I've gone through, it has all been worth it to see her happy. She calls me 'mum' and my parents 'nanny' and 'granpy'. She even brought me a ring with 'mum' on it. It makes it all worthwhile. She is such a lovely child and she is so thoughtful.

We don't hear from her mother but she has contacted the SSD here. She has sent letters to Noreen but she got so upset that she ripped them up and wants no contact with her at all. She hasn't heard for a while.

I'm not stupid, I know that she is not biologically mine. I know her parents are always going to be there. At the same time, I've got to try to keep it real here. This is Noreen's home. The parents are at the back of my mind but for Noreen I've got to be strong and keep things together. If I fall apart, well, who knows what would happen.

There have been a lot of meetings with social workers. I had to have a police check and tell them about my past. The original social worker, well, I even threatened to throw her out. For a long time, they were saying to Noreen, 'You should really have contact with your parents'. When you are sat there and you've got a child in tears and the social worker is not listening to Noreen or me: it got to the stage when you went round in circles every time they came. They go by their textbook but just because the book insists that every child has contact with their father, it does not mean that you can make that child do it. But it has improved. I have a different social worker now and she brought a new one last week. They are listening and that's all I want them to do. Now she is going about it in a different way and is trying to find out the reasons why Noreen is feeling the way she is.

The social work was helpful when I was in the hostel. They helped me get out quick. The SSD oversees the placement but they can't actually tell us what to do. It's like this residence order, I have to do it myself because it is a private fostering agreement. I have to see my own solicitor. Obviously, until she is 18, her parents have parental responsibility but I want some security. The social workers are supposed to come every eight weeks and every six months they are supposed to hold a review. The present one is in two parts. The first part was here because Noreen didn't want to go all the way to their office as it is in the town which has too many memories for her plus the fact that she does not want to be in the same room as her father. I was there, Noreen and two social workers. Noreen was quite open with them and told them where she wants to be. It went pretty well and it was good to talk. The next part will be with the social worker, Noreen's father, me, and someone who takes the minutes. I say to the social workers that if Noreen gets to 12 or 13 and wants to go back to her dad then she is free to go. OK, I'd be upset but I want her to be happy and safe and do what she wants. The social workers have wavered, have moved the goal posts but all I want is for Noreen to be happy.

Mrs Johnson

Mrs Johnson was born in Germany where she started looking after other people's children. After moving to England, she has fostered 32 West African children.

I am a German and married an airman. I've been in England 36 years. I have four of my own children, all grown up. Even in Germany, where my first two were born, I had my sister's girl since she was ten days old and we brought her up until she was married. I always wish people would drop a baby on my doorstep. I just love babies.

I had trained as a children's nurse in Germany and worked with premature babies. When we moved to England, they insisted that I take the exams again and I said I would not do that. My sister had done fostering for the council in Germany, mostly coloured children, and there was one Ghana family who wanted their child to go to school in England. Then they rang me from London. One day I was at my work, my daughter was visiting, and when I got in she said, 'You'll never guess who came today, you have a baby now'. She had brought him on Christmas Eve, he was 14 months old. I had no idea at what stage of eating and drinking he was at. I had to go round neighbours and borrow nappies until after Christmas. That was how I started. He stayed until he was three.

Most of my children have been from Ghana. Two sets were Nigerian. Most of them are somehow related. The parents are in London and are students or single parents or divorced mothers. There is more private fostering in London, most of it unofficial. I have heard of people with ten children. Usually they stay until they are two or three. Once they are able to feed themselves, clothe themselves and are clean, they come and get them. I do miss them when they go. It is very hard for us to understand. In Ghana, particularly in the country areas and where there are strong tribal connections, when a young woman has a baby, a maiden aunt or grandmother looks after the child. So when the parents come over here, they have no idea how to look after a baby in the way that we do because we learn from our own parents. Three of the families have gone back to Ghana. I keep in touch with some. Last year I had a letter from the second child I had. She is 16 now and wrote out of the blue. She was at college in Ghana and involved in the church.

I was divorced. My husband was very prejudiced, he didn't mind me doing it for white but not coloured children. I never had trouble from neighbours. Once my daughter and I were shopping in town and there were two old ladies. I heard one say to the other, 'Look at her, she got nigger babies, why can't she take white ones?' That was the only time I had nasty remarks. My youngest boy was eight when I fostered and he used to walk in front or behind me when we went shopping. I queried that and he said, 'No, I don't mind the children but what about if some of my classmates see me and think you have married a coloured man?' After a while, he didn't mind.

Most parents do visit regularly while I have the babies. This is especially important with babies because they don't remember that long. It is hard for eight, nine or ten month old babies to be taken away by their parents for a week and they scream. But when they come back, they scream again. For that reason

I say, 'Don't come and visit in the first month, let the child settle in. You can ring four or five times a day, don't mind that'.

Payment is arranged with the parents. Two sets of parents did not pay. One went to Ghana for a couple of months and I had to go to the DHSS and they advanced me the money and when the mother repaid me, I returned it. But you can't do that any more.

I charged £85 a month when I started. As the children get older, I expect the parents to provide coats and shoes. The parents keep the child benefit. SSDs pay a lot more to their foster parents.

I had one set of Nigerian brothers. The first was seven when he came. When he knew his mother was coming, he was dreadful. He would sit stiff and he would not cuddle her and she would not kiss him. He had behaviour problems at school and she would say, 'If you don't behave yourself, I send you back to Nigeria.' He tried to be good but he couldn't relax.

I had one girl, she was four when she came. The parents were asylum seekers, he had been in the airforce. When the girl came back from a stay with her parents, she always had big burns. They would say, 'She fell on the poker'. Once she had a burn on top of her foot and across her back. Obviously I had to take her to the doctor and they wanted to take it further. I managed to persuade them to leave her with me. Then I had a word with some of the parents' relatives so that they could tell them that I did not think she accidentally burnt herself and if she came like that again, action had to be taken. Funnily enough, she never burnt herself after that.

The last two boys I had were brothers. One was six months old when he came and when he was three I took his six weeks old brother. I kept them for another five years and when they left I was deeply, deeply upset.

I still have Sonia. I took her when she was eight and now she is 15. Her mother was a nurse who worked nights and her father had a dry-cleaning business. I knew from the start that she would stay until she finished school. She is a part of our family and my children look upon her as a sister. She comes on holiday with me. She also goes on holiday to Germany with one of my daughters. She has flown to America twice to see an uncle there. I've had no trouble with Sonia, she has a circle of girl friends.

At school, she is weak in maths, average in other subjects. She is very good at sport. She would like to open her own health spa so she is doing GCSE sport. Her first choice was air stewardess but her mother did not like it so she changed her mind. Last year, she was the town's carnival princess and her photo was in the paper.

There was a time when Sonia wrote my name on her books at school and she wanted very much that I adopt her. She was afraid that her mum would take her back again. Her mother agreed to the adoption but at the last minute she changed her mind. I did try to apply for a residence order but again her mother had to sign it but she did not. Now her mother says, I can have her and I say, 'It's a bit late now'. But Sonia uses her own surname now.

She does not want to go back to her parents. When she was a baby, they used to have her for short periods. They used to pick her up on Fridays and then ring on a Saturday, 'We're bringing her back, she's screaming'. Then her parents divorced and, since she was ten or 11, she has visited her mother on a regular basis. She last saw her dad two years ago. Every holiday she goes to her mum and they are getting on all right now. Sonia went to Ghana four years ago and did not like it. Then she went two years ago and enjoyed it. She is older and can stand up for herself, isn't over-awed and can speak the language a bit. But she would not want to live there.

I have had few problems. I am affectionate with children. I cuddle them to death. My own grown up children are the same and always give me a kiss and a cuddle. I have learned to look after coloured children. You have to cream their skin daily and also their hair. Boys keep their hair short so that you can comb it quick. The girls' hair is plaited because they want girls to have long hair. I can't do this so they have to wait until their mothers come. I had to learn that coloured children have smaller bladders so they are harder to train to get dry, you have to take them more often to the potty.

When I took my first foster child I rang the social workers and asked about it. I have to register every child. First of all I had a very good social worker. There were no rules about private fostering then but I said I wanted something definite. After a while, she said, 'I can see you cope well and we are very short-staffed, if you have a problem give me a ring, otherwise I will keep visits to the minimum'. She would come every three months for a small child. Then she retired and there seems a new one every year. Sonia got on well with the previous social worker. She would say, 'Do you mind if I meet her after school and have a cup of coffee in town with her?' I did not object for sometimes children want to say something but not in front of the foster mother. I did not like it when another social worker sent some forms to the school, asking if Sonia had any problems, without telling me. I do not need the social workers but it is right that they should check. Once I had five children under one year and the social worker said this was too much. I am now 60 and I am not sure if they would say I could take more after Sonia.

Mrs Helen Mitchell

Mrs Helen Mitchell took in her foster daughter when she was eight and she stayed until she was 17. They are still in close and happy contact.

The child I took was my sister's girl .She was an alcoholic and stayed with a drunken partner. When they had fights, Molly would run away and come to me. They lived from hand-to-mouth in sublet accommodation. They wouldn't pay the rent and had to run off in the middle of the night. Molly was their only child but they separated before she was born so she has never had any contact with him. Sometimes my sister would go back to stay with our mum who was on drugs and I can remember Molly as a toddler saying, 'Oh, grannie's full of the drugs'.

When Molly was eight, her mother went to jail for social security fraud. Nobody came to tell her what had happened so she came round to me and said, 'My mum's not come back'. I kept her for a few days expecting her mother to come and say, 'What's going on here? Where's my daughter?' When she did not appear, I made enquiries and discovered that she was in jail.

For a wee while it was a bit much for my husband because he was young, we had three small children and we were not well off. I didn't want money to keep her. I was afraid that if we said we couldn't afford to keep her then she would be taken into care. Her mother never paid a penny, never a thank you: in fact she had the cheek to criticise. I had gone to the police to find out what had happened to her mother and they put social services on to the case and I got an allowance: but she was not in care. In fact we saw little of social workers. I used to say to my husband that we could have sold Molly into white slavery and they would not have known. They came about once a year. I was glad they came and would have been glad of any advice but we never had any problems.

She was like a wee mother with my boys and she still adores them. There was some jealousy when they got to teens because she was the only girl.

She was exceptionally well behaved, amazing when you read about all these children needing counselling now. If I said 'don't do it' that was it. Even then she appreciated what we had done for her. In her early teens, I worried a bit about which way she was going to go but not for long.

In every way she has been my daughter, she's a lovely daughter. She always kept her own surname. She called us aunt and uncle. She was eight when she came and we didn't want her to make too many adjustments to her life. We always treated her as an equal and never spoke down to her.

We tried to keep contact with her mother but she kept moving. We did not always know where she was but when we found her we went round. She never troubled to come and see her daughter. I was glad that she didn't make a nuisance of herself and put on a show that she wanted her child back, which she obviously didn't.

It surprised me that this did not upset Molly. My own mother was a drug addict before drug addicts were even thought off. In those days it was purple hearts and lentizol, which was a sleeping pill. When she died, the post mortem said that they had melted her brain. I would have always gone back to my own mother no matter what she had done. But Molly didn't. I said to her, 'Your mother's your mother, I'm only a stand-in, you've still got that strong blood relationship with her'. And she would say, 'No, no, no. I haven't. I've only got pity for her.' At her mothers' funeral, by this time Molly was 38, she said, 'I would have been really upset if it had been someone who mattered'. I used to ask whether she would like to get in touch with her dad but she said she was not interested and she's never set her eyes on him.

She did quite well at school, got some O levels and was good at design. She went into office work. When she was 17, she moved south to a girl she had been friendly with at school. Her family invited her to move to South Africa with them. She went and lasted about three months and wanted home again. Dad wrote and said that as soon as we can get the fare together you are coming home and that wherever I am that is where your home is. My husband was a driver until he was made redundant and then he worked as a porter at the hospital. But he made sure she got back. After that she went south again and made a very good marriage. They've built up a business between them, got a beautiful big house and two lovely children. The first one was called after me. My middle boy moved down to be near Molly. All my boys are now married with children so we like to have a family get together.

We gave her a lot of love but anything we ever did for her we've had back tenfold. She's a lovely, attentive girl. She always talks of this as home. Not a day goes by when she does not phone.

Mrs Betty Sutton

Mrs Betty Sutton is a lone parent with three children and dependent upon social security benefits. She had no previous fostering experience when she took in a friend of her son.

I had a mixed race marriage and lived in North Africa. It broke up and I came back with my three sons, now aged seven, 13 and 17. My middle son had a friend at school, he was 13 or 14. He'd been to our house a couple of times and he told me that he was leaving home or getting thrown out. He told me that he had phoned the Child Help Line and given them my name and address. The Help Line must have contacted the social services for somebody phoned us from there. I didn't ask too many questions as to what was going on as it was traumatic for the boy and he didn't want people prying. They asked would I be willing to take him for that night and they would see about something the following day. I said that was fine. I gathered that his family was not really interested in him. The social workers then phoned back to say he would be staying a few days. This was just before Christmas and apparently the social workers had three or four children to place. He stayed for a few days and I felt sorry for him and I contacted the social services and said he could stay at least until the new year. They said it would have to be an arrangement made with his dad. I got in touch with the father. He didn't know me and was willing for him to stay with me and on the financial side asked if I would accept £30 a week. After that I had no contact with the father. His real mother was living somewhere else. I got paid three times altogether over three months and he would just hand in an envelope at the door. No phone calls asking how he was. The father didn't want to know him at Christmas so I had to buy him Christmas things. A couple of days after Christmas day, his stepmother did bring him some presents but didn't want to speak to him.

There was little back-up from his family or the social workers. We did have one meeting between the social workers, the school, his father, the boy and myself. The social workers seemed to be getting more at the father's background and showing how this made for behavioural problems with his son. The father then said a rude word and walked out. I'm on social security myself and, when I didn't get money, I got in touch with the social services and occasionally they'd give me some food vouchers. Financially I was getting in a mess because I kept on expecting to be paid for him and the social services said they would take over payment for him. That never happened. The only support was at school where he got counselling. Eventually he got a social worker. She was only part-time. I had no help whatsoever. Well, they did get me some bunk beds and that was it.

I had to let him go after a few months. He didn't like my youngest who was six. One of my other sons was getting into trouble with him. I do have feelings for him, I took him into my own home. But my own family had to come first. So he went into care and to a foster home. He seems quite happy but is running amok. He goes to school, goes home, has tea, and then comes straight round to my house. He's run away a couple of times and come back to me. So the council foster parents are getting money for old rope.

This is a small estate but a lot of children get thrown out by their parents. They go from friends to friends or people take them in. It is so different from abroad where I lived for 15 years. There people looked after their own.

Chapter 9: The Private Fostering Professionals

Iris Amoah

Iris Amoah was born and educated in Ghana before coming to Britain. She is now team manager of the task-centred fostering team in Newham Social Services Department.

Having graduated as an economics teacher, I taught for two years and went on to do a masters degree in regional planning. I was married and had a son. I was aware of fostering in Ghana. When my parents were changing jobs, I lived with my aunt for about a year. I had another aunt who was the head of a teacher training college who opened her home to a number of children of friends and former students of the college.

In 1980, I came to England and worked as an unqualified social worker in Leicester before training as a social worker. It was in Leicester that I became aware of private fostering. Children were placed with total strangers. I had contact with some students who used private fostering and tried to raise their awareness of its impact on their children. I had four children and worked full-time but, in the interests of my children, I asked for a reduction in hours so that I could look after them.

I then worked as a social worker for the Nigerian High Commission and my main responsibility was private fostering. I liaised with the African Families Advisory Service of the Save the Children Fund and with the International Social Service as well as with SSDs in London and in the shires where Nigerian children were placed. I assessed the needs of parents and children and helped them to cope with the change in culture which impacted on their child care practices. I liaised with local authorities and private foster carers and promoted an understanding of Nigerian culture and appropriate ways of meeting the needs of children. Having done some direct work with the children in foster homes, I was able to work towards rehabilitating children back to parents in Nigeria.

Part of my role at the Nigerian High Commission was to promote a better understanding of parents' legal responsibilities as stated in legislation and to raise their awareness regarding some of the complications of leaving their children in private foster homes for too long. Some of the parents acted appropriately and removed their children so they could care for them. I wrote court reports where parents and private foster carers battled over the custody of the private foster children. We lost three cases out of 12 but I was, however, aware of many instances up and down the country where the parents lost their children to the private foster carers.

I enjoyed working with SSDs, particularly Hampshire, Swindon and Shropshire. They worked in partnership with the High Commission and had procedures in place. They liaised appropriately to meet the needs of Nigerian children in their care. Hampshire went further, through a survey, to explore the needs of birth parents living in London and how they could be supported in order to keep their children in London. All was going well when, after two years, I was informed by the High Commission—following restructuring—that my services were no longer required. In my view, there were other reasons which I would rather not talk about.

Having left the High Commission, I worked as an agency social worker at Camden SSD in their looked after children team. My responsibilities did not cover private fostering but I used to see Nigerian children placed with white families. I was not aware of any monitoring of private fostering. Private foster carers do operate in the boroughs but not as much as in the shires. Parents who live in London tend to place their children outside London.

From Camden, I came to Newham as a senior practitioner in the task-centred fostering team. My duties did not cover private fostering. In the past Newham had a post which undertook work with private fostering and made an effort to raise the profile. This is no longer the case. I met one private foster carer and persuaded her to inform the area social work team. I got a social worker to confirm that she did so but I do not believe that any visits were made. Because of my experience, I have been given permission to attend the meetings of the BAAF Private Fostering Practice Issues Group and the Health Visitors Private Fostering Special Interest Group. I have been asked to do a report on private fostering for the borough, including what other London SSDs are doing, and I have just completed this.

Private fostering worries me because the children are living away from home and their parents do not really understand the set-up in which they are placing their children. I am concerned about racism within private foster homes. If people want to use private fostering placements, then I'd prefer if it was very time limited because of the impact on the children. Children always internalise bad experiences which affect their relationships with their parents. The parents are distressed at the thought of losing their children. The children find it difficult to deal with their rejection and abandonment. When the children have an identity crisis they may not want anything to do with Nigeria which upsets the parents. When I was at the High Commission, I worked with some parents who had been privately fostered themselves and, as a result, feel unable to address their own needs let alone their children's needs. They had been damaged by being fostered and it is heartbreaking to see them feeling so isolated and not knowing where to go to share their experiences and to ask for help.

Some private foster carers may be genuinely interested in children but we ought to be working with them in ways which enhance their knowledge and skills, to let them know that the children are not theirs and will one day return to their parents. They need to work in partnership with parents in the best interests of the children.

Some Nigerian students continue to use private fostering but the majority are now working. Day care does not appear to fit in with their life styles because many are working unsociable hours. They want a form of care that is flexible and provides continuity until the children are five plus and are at school and more independent. Private fostering frees them to concentrate on studies or jobs. I was aware that some children were sexually abused but, in my experience I did not deal with children who were known to have suffered physical and sexual abuse, although there was racial and emotional abuse. In one home, I made my first visit to a boy of about five. The house had a massive black dog and he was terrified of it. The carers did not see it as a problem. Basically they were saying, 'Why should you be scared of yourself?' In his room, there was almost nothing except one poster. You get the impression that some of these children are not seen as human beings. In another home, the child touched my hair, ran away then came back to touch my hands. She kept looking at me straight in the eye. When I was about to leave, she didn't want to go to the carer and cried.

The time has come for private foster carers to be registered. SSDs must be pro-active in finding out where children are. They must then decide whether the private foster children should be deemed as 'in need' or not. If referrals go direct to area social work teams, then they must liaise with the fostering units for they have expertise about fostering. But every private foster child needs a social worker.

It is important that the parents should come forward for advice and social workers should encourage them to see placements as very time-limited. The parents also need someone to talk with but who they are where they go to is the question.

Heather Clacy

A qualified and experienced social worker, Heather Clacy is a private fostering social worker in Kent Social Services.

After a degree in sociology at Leeds Poly, I was seconded by Barnsley SSD to take the social work course at Bristol University. On returning I was in a generic social work team before moving to Kent SSD. I took time out for my family and then returned. I obtained a job with Kent as social worker (private fostering).

I am responsible for Mid Kent, there is a similar worker in East Kent but in the West of the county, which has three area teams, private fostering is dealt with on a local team basis. I think the work is done better by one person as they then deal with the number of cases that gives them expertise in private fostering but assessments should go to the fostering panel so that they are scrutinised by a wider range of people.

Most of the private children in Mid Kent are in Ashford. When a referral comes in, I look at the foster carer's suitability which involves meeting them and their family, getting their background, carrying out statutory checks. I see the child and get from the carer as much information about them as possible. But I do not see the natural parents unless they live locally. If I consider the carers suitable and there are no issues, then my report is endorsed by my manager and I then visit the children regularly. If there is a difficulty, say the carers are disqualified persons, then the decision is made at area director level. It does not go to the home finding panel in the way that applications to foster for the local authority go, although I think this should happen. I had one carer who was disqualified because a member of the household had criminal convictions. I informed the mother and she removed the child. If this had not happened, it would probably have gone along the child protection route. The foster carers were informed of their right to appeal but they accepted it. There have been other instances where the foster carers are not ideal, we would not accept them as local authority carers, but we allow it on the basis that the parents have made the choice but they also have to be assessed as suitable to privately foster.

At the moment there are only 12 private foster children in this district. The numbers have diminished for a variety of reasons. One is that there are now better day care facilities. It may be that the message is getting through to parents that it is not always good for their children to be fostered. Perhaps the private carers here now know that I am coming around regularly and that we are prepared to take action. This may have deterred some from continuing for certainly some previous carers have dropped out. Economically, more women who might have been private foster carers are getting jobs outside the home.

It is the number of West African foster children which is diminishing most. The ones I have got have parents working in London. They work long hours with shift work and need to make provision for their children. Often the children return to them when they are 11 and go to secondary school. Another group, which I think has hidden numbers and needs more publicity, are white children estranged from their own families and living with friends. Occasionally there are young children with attachment problems with their own parents who are handed on to friends of the family. This can often be a prelude to them being accommodated by the local authority or even adoption being considered.

A West African girl was placed with elderly foster parents who have done private fostering for 40 years. She came directly from Nigeria as her parents thought there were better opportunities in Britain. They are now in London and the girl was due to return to them. The girl persuaded her mum to let her stay as she is happy here, as her friends are here, and as she was just starting secondary school. She sees her mum about once a month and has contact during the school holidays. She has encountered a couple of incidents of racial abuse which her foster carer has tried to help her with. But it can't be properly addressed for she is a black girl with a white carer in a predominantly white area. There are two other black private foster children in the home. The woman does care for the children but there are questions about promoting identity and culture. The girl is going through a difficult patch behaviourally at school. The carer is struggling and may say to her, 'If you don't behave, I'll send you back'.

I have never met the parents of this girl, I've only had telephone contact. I have met other parents from London when my visit coincided with them visiting the foster home. I am not encouraged to make trips to London to see parents.

In other situations, teenagers are estranged from mum and dad and go to live with a neighbour. Sometimes mum and dad are not happy with this and after a while they return home.

The private foster carers often regard me with some suspicion. They see us as the authorities who remove children. Some of my relationships are difficult because in the past some of the carers, for various reasons, have been unwilling to co-operate with the authorities, they want to do things on their own because it is a private arrangement. They don't see the need for us to monitor the children, although there is a grudging acceptance with some.

I visit the children the number of times according to the legal requirement but more often if there are problems. I do see the children on their own and some carers are more co-operative than others about this. I talk with them about what is happening at home, at school. They do know that I am making sure that they are all right in the foster home and some joke about me seeing that they are not beaten up.

The notification system does not work. I can think of only one private foster carer who lets me know when a child is going to arrive. Mostly you only find out after the child has arrived. I find out through other professionals and through visiting the home to see one child and they say, 'Oh, by the way, we've had so and so'. And you don't always learn when or why the child is leaving.

We have got a number of language schools in the area and children coming on cultural exchanges. Some let me know of their existence and then we can do checks. I have contacted other language schools and they tell me they do not have anyone placed for more than 28 days. Of course, if they are staying more than 28 days, it is possible to get round the regulations by just moving them somewhere else.

Within the department, there is not a lot of clarity about private fostering. I try to spread knowledge of the regulations. I speak with health visitors and give them information about private fostering so that they can refer cases. It is almost impossible to get money from the department to spend on private fostering, on the children, natural parents, carers. I tried to get a grant for a bus ticket to school for one child to save her walking to school but it was not accepted. All private foster children are designated as 'in need' but it is still difficult to get money for them. Private fostering is not a priority so it is still difficult to obtain resources. This is another argument for not putting private fostering to local teams because it would get low priority as against other cases.

Private fostering is not a good enough system. Proper registration of carers is needed as is training for them. The existing government had the opportunity to take the initiative but it did not do so. It is the cultural side which worries me most, the lack of contact private foster children have with children from a similar cultural background. The children who have more contact with their own parents do better. But others are going to lose their language and much more. Some carers make negative remarks about black families in front of the children. The other worrying factor is the lack of a plan for a child so that they have no idea how long they are going to be there and some do not see their parents very often. I feel a lack of control. I can't really do much about it unless I go down the child protection route. I can only chip away.

Beverley Clarke

Beverley Clarke came to Britain from Jamaica as a teenager. She is currently a health visitor team adviser in Community Health South London NHS Trust (Lambeth Borough), and is chair of the Community Practitioners' Health Visiting Association Special Interest Group for Private Fostering.

Born in Jamaica, I came to this country in my teens. I trained at Lewisham hospital as a state registered nurse and then did midwifery before qualifying as a health visitor in 1986. Since then, I have mainly worked in Lambeth.

Private fostering came to my attention whilst working as a health visitor in 1987-88. Professionals like health visitors have always had concerns about privately fostered children. We would do a new birth visit to a baby and then find they have disappeared at the follow-up visit. We might see the parents and they would say, 'Oh, they are away with a nanny'. We'd ask for the address but they would reply, 'We don't know but we know how to get there'. The children might appear back on our caseload two or three years later with problems of poor language development, problems with their identity and behavioural difficulties. In some cases, parents may then consult with their general practitioner for depression because they find it difficult to cope with the children's behaviour. Some of the children might become subject of child protection procedures because of the mother's inability to cope with them.

My first involvement came about when a local mother placed her two year old daughter with a private foster carer whose own children had been taken into care by the local authority. The carer's older son and a friend were swinging this little girl in a playground and she fell and broke her arm. The SSD became involved and placed her in a children's home. It was my task to visit the mother and explain how important it was for her to try and have her daughter back home. All she could say was that the baby was always clinging and crying and she couldn't cope. She was also pregnant with her second child. Her husband was a student and she was working long hours. I tried to get her to recognise the needs of her daughter and her responsibilities as a parent. She had a friend visiting her at the time and she was keen to know how she could get her children into the children's home! With perseverance and coaxing, the mother did eventually have her daughter home and we worked together to develop a bond between them. I still see this mother on the estate and the last time she remarked that her daughter was so traumatised by her experience that she would never stay with anybody else again.

There have been many other cases. One client, who was about to use private fostering, followed my advice and informed the SSD. I advised her to visit beforehand to see the environment where her child would be living. She did so and had the shock of her life. She found the house very dirty and the private foster carer suffering from a skin condition. She opted to use child minding services locally.

The majority of private fostering arrangements I have seen are West African, especially Nigerian. The parents often work very long hours on low wages and find this to be the most viable option for the care of their children. But they do not know the effects, short term and long term, on their children. These children are trans-racially placed in areas where there are few or no black people like themselves. So there are no black role models for them. When they return home, they have difficulties relating to their black parents. They lack insight and knowledge about their culture and identity. There is confusion as they get older and realise they are different. They are left in emotional turmoil. I will always remember doing a new birth visit to a young Nigerian woman and raising the issue of private fostering. She told me she was privately fostered and never saw a black person until she came to London. She was so frightened by the experience that she ran and went straight into a car. She was never told any thing positive about black people by her foster carer. She found the whole experience so traumatic that she would never send 'her dog' to be privately fostered.

Not all West African parents who use private fostering are students now. They are basically working class people who believe that placing their children in private fostering gives them a better start. Sometimes they are studying but it is not like 1950s when students had funds from their governments to support them.

Private fostering is no longer confined to West African children. The categories are changing. Chinese parents are now placing their children with private foster carers. Language students when they stay with families for over 28 days are privately fostered. There are white teenagers who move out of their homes to live with friends. Children that are brought into this country for back door adoption are privately fostered, also those from countries where there are crises. I have had asylum seekers, awaiting their cases to be heard and wanting to work, wishing to have their children privately fostered and I have persuaded them not to place their children in private foster care. I am sure that many of these children are missing and no one is aware of their whereabouts.

We had a seminar in 1998 at the former Lambeth Healthcare Trust and it was surprising how many social workers were not aware of the definition of private fostering and the responsibilities of SSDs. It is therefore not surprising that they do not know how many private foster children exist. My task has been to try to raise the awareness of private fostering not just amongst clients but also professionals. I went to Nigeria in 1990 to a conference organised by the Nigerian government and Save the Children where raising awareness received a high profile. Following the conference, we set up the Community Practitioners' Health Visitors' Association Special Interest Group for Private Fostering. Members include health visitors, school nurses and social workers and representatives from the Nigerian High Commission and the Department of Health. It has produced good practice guides for health visitors and school nurses. We received funding from the Department of Health for a guide for private foster carers called *Caring for Other People's Children* which can be used by all carers with black and mixed race children. We want to ensure that, through good practice, clients are identified and appropriate information and intervention is given to ensure relevant services to meet their needs in an ethnically sensitive way.

Health visitors are often the first professionals to identify private foster children. We see clients in the antenatal period and are therefore able to discuss and advise about local day care facilities. This is an ideal opportunity to discuss and raise the potential hazard of private fostering arrangements with those who are likely to use it. Many tell us about their friends who have used this form of care and are happy with it. Although we need to be careful not to impinge on their right to choose, we have a duty to ensure that children are safeguarded and protected. It is a very sensitive area and needs to be managed with care.

When we identify the children, we use our skills to make an holistic assessment and this includes knowing when to refer to another agency. With this assessment framework now on-line for use by all agencies, it will enable more information to be gathered about the child-carer in assessing the needs of the child. This should reduce the number of children who are not assessed appropriately because of poor knowledge about their histories.

For a long time, social workers and health visitors have tended to work in response to crises. They have a fear about child protection so we are too busy reacting to that. Most people who use private fostering do so in response to child care and poverty needs. If we were working in a preventative way and addressed these needs we would avoid some of the subsequent tragedies. The

Anna Climbie case has caught the media eye but there are more children that have died in private foster homes than is recognised. If we are responsible for the welfare of children then the services should be there to support them. And this can only happen if practitioners are competent in this area of work. If more resources were allocated to prevention then it would save millions of pounds that is now spent on therapy that often will not make a difference to that child's life in the long term. If you look at penal and mental health services, you see that the number of black, young men in their institutions is far greater than the proportion in the population. Has anyone traced their histories or their childhoods?

Health and social services should work together to provide a service for children who are or who may become private foster children. Their needs are as great as those of children looked after by local authorities. This was shown in the review by Sir William Utting and he recognised private foster children as a very vulnerable group. He recommended registration of private foster carers and this would be the biggest way of preventing tragedies. Registration will weed out the bad carers. It will also strengthen the good ones and raise the standard of care for these children. Those who have gone through rigorous training and various checks will not want Mrs Bloggs down the road to do it if she is unregistered. All the child care groups lobbied for registration to be brought in and were disappointed when the government refused. The majority of children are black. If we were talking about 6–9,000 white children would this situation have been allowed to continue for so long? Institutional racism prevails.

When I started the work in Lambeth, I had good involvement with the SSD. I met together with the manager who had the lead in private fostering to work out policies and protocols. I put a system in place whereby health visitors would inform me about local private foster carers and I would transfer the information to social services. The social workers would then visit these carers to do their assessment. Those children put in private foster homes in other areas would also be notified to me. Recently things have changed and there is no longer a lead officer in private fostering. I have written to the Head of Children Resources and the Chief Executive because I do need to renew the work that was done over the years. Similarly, the London boroughs, which have the parents, no longer work closely with the home counties where the children are placed. The work in the past was good but now it has become more difficult.

The Department of Health has announced a private fostering public awareness campaign following the Utting Review. The trouble is that so much is happening in health and social services that private fostering continues to be a low priority. Yet this unregulated service continues, with the majority of local authorities saying they have none in their area, and these children remain vulnerable with no agency overseeing them to ensure their health and well-being is safeguarded.

I know a couple of cases where the white private foster carers have wanted residence orders for their black private foster children. Parents are ignorant to the fact that after three years the carers can apply for orders. A number of parents have lost their children through the courts in custody battles because of this ignorance. To the African cultural belief, the family cannot be written out of the child's life by legal means.

The children are always caught in the middle of the court cases. The decisions made always worry me for often it is felt that the child is better off with the carers rather than their parents. Those with responsibilities for making these decisions lack insight into the long term effect on these children in terms of their heritage, their culture, their identity. These are the children who end up confused as adults. We need to go back to prevention so that these children and their families have quality care from the outset. There is more recognition now that we need to be more pro-active in preventative work, especially in light of the government initiative in supporting families.

We also need to encourage more black carers. Few black people come forward to do so, or to foster for the local authority or to adopt, because they feel the system negates them. The people who do the assessments need to be more sensitive to black people and not shut the door at the first hurdle. Of course, there must be basic criteria for entry by which you can weed out those who are not suitable. But there are many potential carers out there amongst this population who, with the right support and adequate training, can meet the needs of these children. There is a need for the same number of minority ethnic carers as minority ethnic children.

More trained private foster carers are needed because the numbers of private foster children are underestimated. The numbers that local authorities collected for government were far below those estimated by the African Family Advisory Service. This confusion over collecting statistics used to go on over child minding. Then child minders became regulated. The result was that the number of minders was collected while people received a much better service. This is not to say that unregistered minding does not go on but parents now have an option. But private fostering is almost unchecked so how can some local authorities say they do not have any?

Change has to come to prevent another death like Anna Climbie, and this can only happen when this service is regulated.

Angus Geddes

Angus Geddes has been a social worker for over 20 years. At present he is fostering development officer in the family placement team in the social services section of Swindon Borough Council. He and his wife are also local authority foster parents.

As a student, I was sent to inspect a private foster home. There was an elderly woman in a dirty house with two Nigerian twins aged between two and three, strapped in a pram. They could not walk and a health visitor agreed that their development was impaired. We also discovered that the woman had TB. The children suddenly disappeared and presumably went back to their parents. I had other private foster cases and so became interested in a system which was full of holes.

I worked as a social worker in an area team in a county SSD and ended up carrying most of the private fostering cases for the part of the town I covered. In 1985, the department obtained some Section 11 money under the Local Government Act of 1966 for work with ethnic minority groups and I set up a specialist project in Swindon to look at mainly West African private foster children. I took on every private fostering case in Swindon. The numbers were in the 80s and later settled down to the 40s for five to six years.

I set up a system. If a new referral of a private foster child came in, the child was allocated to a field social worker to carry out the visits. I know that some departments give all responsibility to a private fostering specialist but I prefer an area field social worker to be involved. If things go wrong in a private fostering then that child is more easily integrated into the area child care set-up. Private foster carers were allocated to a family placement officer to do the police checks and make an assessment.

This assessment was then approved (or not) by a manager who would record that the arrangement appeared to be suitable. When assessing carers, it is fairly easy to judge the environment, the stair gate, the fire detectors etc. The difficult bit is assessing their attitudes towards children. The private foster carers who don't want to work with you are probably the most worrying. We probably accept a lower level of care than for local authority carers because the parents have chosen them. The local authority has access to the carers' history and can do police checks. The local authority can advise the natural parents but, in the end, their decision counts for a lot. If the carer was a disqualified person then we would get the solicitor's department to issue a prohibition notice. The natural parents would be advised to remove the child. If the parents did not know where to put their child then they could seek further help from the local authority. In one case, a couple of private foster children were placed on a Sunday and on the Monday I got the couple to fill in police check forms. When I returned to the office, the male carer phoned to say that he had a number of convictions, including that of a Schedule 1 nature, but his wife did not know about them. I said he had better return the children home which they did within the week.

Since the Children Act (1989), I always recommend that a private foster child is a child 'in need' unless there are grounds otherwise. This has implications for the department spending money on the child so sometimes the reaction is deathly silence. But private foster children are potentially some of the most vulnerable children in the country.

In my opinion, private foster carers fall into three categories. First, those you can prohibit because they are disqualified persons. Second, those who are really interested in fostering and are willing to co-operate with us for the benefit of the children. Third, those who don't want anything to do with the social services. These are the most worrying because you are not sure what their agenda is.

We developed groups for white private foster carers looking after black children. They were mainly staffed by black women and we observed that some black children were frightened at the sight of black adults. They lived in white areas and rarely saw black adults. Those who did have regular contact with them seemed to have fewer anxieties. We had a small private fostering budget and I raised £1,000 from local charities for toys for the foster families to use. The carers who were involved with the groups came to know us very well. They appreciated it and began to tell me of any new placements in the area. Also, after about four years, West African parents would ring me up and say they were thinking of placing a child with Mrs So and So and seek my opinion. So the notification system began to work. It was very successful and some of the carers later became local authority foster carers.

Even before the Children Act (1989), I got parents and foster carers to make placement agreements. It was a discussion about the finances, the child's needs, what to do about health, visiting patterns etc. It was rarely written down but it worked well. Also I would meet parents at the railway station and take them to the foster home. So you got a rapport with all the adults involved. Most of the West African children went back at three years or five years. It was fairly rare for them to stay long term.

I continued in this role until 1991 when the funding ran out and the county decided not to continue the project as it was not considered a priority. I was stopped from supervising private fostering and one manager would not let me use the family centre to continue the group for private foster carers. I moved into the family placement team and the private fostering cases were redistributed amongst all the social workers and interest declined. This continued until 1998 when Swindon became a unitary authority and I stayed with its family placement team. I am now primarily concerned with children looked after by the local authority but I also work in fostering development and one aspect of that is to put private fostering back on the agenda. My recommended system is that a new private foster child would be picked up by the intake team who might hand them on to a long term field social worker. A new foster carer should be assessed by the family placement team and I am recommending that the decision to approve or not be made not by a manager but by a panel—which would be useful if you got into a court situation where you wanted to prohibit someone because the panel would have a base line of experience.

Our computer picks up only two to three private foster children whereas I know of several others. I can't believe that if I had 80 West African children here in 1985 then we have not got any in 2001. In recent years, I've worked with teenagers and came across a number who ended up as children looked after by the local authority but who had previously been private foster children. Typical is the 15 year old who goes to live with the parents of a boy or girl friend or the 14 year old who falls out with their parents. These were not recorded as private foster children. We have a number of South-Eastern European refugee children in town and I have been trying to find out who the younger ones are living with. If there are 20–30 private foster children in Swindon, which seems a reasonable assumption, this is a quarter of the number of local authority children in foster homes.

Private fostering is always a bit of a secret. When I was a new social worker, the Central Office of Information used to distribute leaflets about private fostering. They stopped. When magazines like *The Lady* and *Nursery World* took adverts for private foster children, at least you knew where to look for them. It then went underground. So any government awareness campaign must be a good thing. Local authorities are also supposed to publicise private fostering and we have made some efforts to inform the public and professionals to report them but it has not brought one response.

I think Utting was right to recommend registration of private foster carers. The government has backed off, probably because of the financial implications. However, there is an argument that existing legislation is fairly robust but is not applied. That is the real issue. We showed in the 1980s that it is possible to get a core of good private foster carers around you and then they let you know about carers they are worried about. The big danger is when an irresponsible parent places a child with an irresponsible carer, these are the ones who remain hidden.

Brendan McGrath

Brendan McGrath has many years experience with private fostering. He is currently the private fostering co-ordinator with Gloucestershire SSD.

I came from South London. After taking a degree in economics and politics, I got a job in residential social work in Hackney before I did a CQSW. After that I worked in residential social work and intermediate treatment before coming to Gloucestershire as a senior social worker, then as an assistant area manager. Private fostering did occasionally come up, although field social workers knew nothing about it. We had a child care officers' group which did give some thought to it and the registration and inspection unit bravely said they would do it. They tried to get the bones of a policy and information leaflets together. I was redeployed in 1998 and gradually took on private fostering referrals and I am now the private fostering co-ordinator within the inspection and quality assurance group.

First of all I wrote a Policy and Procedures guide for private fostering. It got through our policy board and it was issued in May 2000. It makes clear that the department does recognise its duty to satisfy itself that the welfare of private foster children are being satisfactorily safeguarded and promoted. The department wants to see the same standards applied to private fostering as to local authority fostering.

I take the initial referrals about private fostering. Few people know anything about private fostering so I investigate many children not all of whom are private fosterings. I will usually talk with the natural parents and find that they do want me to check where the children have gone. I had a child whose parents went abroad without a forwarding address. These may not be private fosterings because the parents had abandoned them and the area social work team must decide what to do.

Once I get a referral and establish it is a private fostering, I start to make an assessment about the suitability of the arrangement. I arrange to see the carer and the child. I ask how the arrangement came about and what was its purpose and intended duration. I look at the bedroom, the kitchen and bathroom. I see the birth certificates of the carers, the kind of things we would do for a local authority fostering application. I assess the carers and take checks. However, the report does not go into the same amount of depth as for a local authority fostering. If it is clear that the fostering is long term then I need to go into greater depth. The children's views must be sought. In a number of cases teenagers have initiated private fostering arrangements as an alternative to being accommodated by the local authority. I contact the parents and assess if they are exercising their parental responsibility. The responses of the parents are very varied. Generally, parents welcome contact and want to know that their children are safe and well.

I write a report to my line manager who is the adoption and fostering manager, although it will go to the foster panel soon. The recommendation is about whether we accept the private fostering arrangement. We do not approve or register the carers. We would not accept an arrangement where there was not sufficient accommodation for the child or where the carers were considered unsuitable. We are bringing in a different judgement than for approving local authority foster carers. The overall issue is about what is in the child's best interests. There are cases where the placement is not ideal but, given the child's age and wishes and feelings, I recommend that the department goes along with it. In my report, I state whether I consider the child to be 'in need' under Section 17 of the Children Act (1989) and whether the child would benefit from other services from the local authority. For older children, in particular, I comment on whether I would view the young person as vulnerable if the placement broke down after they were 16, and ask the area team to make a commitment to after care services.

We've never had to deal with a carer who is disqualified from fostering and we have never had to prohibit anyone. There was a case where we thought we'd have to take action but we were able to persuade the parents to make alternative arrangements. Cases are as confusing and complex as any referred to a child care team and, depending on the circumstances, require as much time and skill to find resolutions that are in the child's best interests and acceptable to all concerned. We have never even imposed a requirement on private foster carers. I talk to them and they will usually accept my suggestions, for instance putting in a smoke detector.

Reports are signed by the adoption and fostering manager, who says whether or not the recommendation in the report is accepted. But it is better that it goes to the foster panel. The panel is more open, there is less possibility of collusion, and it may well bring up other issues. Once accepted, the arrangement is added to the department's Index of Private Fostering Arrangements.

Responses from area fieldwork teams are varied. Some cases have social workers allocated, some are held by the duty team, and others have no social work involvement. An assessment report might make a number of recommendations about specific issues. Some teams are very defensive. Conflict can arise when I assess a child as 'in need', and this can have implications for the area budget. Same with after care. Most areas will provide some support, though it is dependent on their budget priorities at the time. I might view that a social worker should be allocated to a case, whereas the team manager has other pressures on allocation.

There are difficulties around where my responsibility ends and those of the area team begin. In one case I was concerned about the fieldwork plan, and it was very much a case of my views not being welcomed. I can think of cases where the area team has given financial support to private foster carers to facilitate a placement, though I cannot recall parents having financial support to facilitate a child returning home. But this does raise the issue about when is a private fostering arrangement more properly viewed as a child looked after. If the department is paying a fee each week to a private foster carer then at what point does the department accept that the child has been accommodated, and that a specific approval fostering assessment would be more appropriate?

I can recall cases where payment from Section 17 has been made to help out with clothing or furniture. In one case the child's mother was resident in a drugs rehab unit. The child stayed with neighbours under a private fostering agreement. He felt embarrassed having to depend upon them for pocket money, and the area agreed to provide it. Sometimes an arrangement arises due to a crisis, and the area provides funding in the short term while carers and parents sort out the funding.

While there is conflict, there are also cases where fieldworkers welcome having an independent assessment of a private fostering arrangement. When I was appointed, I think the area teams thought I would take work away from them. It hasn't: it created more work, as they are now aware of arrangements that were previously hidden.

A key part of my role is to raise awareness of private fostering. I have made presentations to health visitors and school nurses. I've written to schools and this has led to enquiries and referrals. I have targeted professional groups and responses have been mainly positive. The next stage must be to target carers, parents, churches and community groups. We have designed and distributed a range of leaflets. A councillor suggested that we place an article in the various free newspapers distributed by the county councils. We do have financial constraints. We need to advertise in the local press and the cost would come from the existing budget allocation for adoption and fostering.

I have organised workshops on private fostering. Six were run between September and December and three more are planned. A workshop takes a day and a half with 12 places on each course. About a 100 invitations were sent to statutory and voluntary bodies, any groups which have contacts with children and carers. Each workshop contains a cross section of people and looks at the criteria for private fostering, the historical perspective, local policy and procedures, the national picture and case studies. Councillors from the social services committee have also attended. Overall they have stimulated interest because most people can recall a private fostering situation they have met. They might even say, 'Oh, we had a child who stayed for six weeks'.

As more become aware about private fostering so we will get to know what the real figures are. The number of referrals in the county has risen from ten in 1998 to 59 so far in 2000. At the moment there are eight arrangements which have been accepted as private fostering arrangements, ten which were previously accepted but have now ended, and 18 undergoing assessment. They include teenagers living with friends of the families or families of school friends, and younger children placed by parents. Notably there are no West African children. In addition there are certain arrangements which might come under the private fostering arrangements depending on the duration of the placement: 37 host families for language schools, eight host families for children from abroad attending independent schools.

In our county, there are three language schools accredited by the British Council. They take children under 16, mainly in the summer months and mainly from Europe and Japan. There are other schools that say they do not take children under 16. The schools we have contacted have welcomed involvement, and with the agreement of host families we have agreed to undertake local authority checks, even if the placement is less than 28 days.

There are also 'Summer Schools' which, I understand, can be set up by anyone. An agent arranges for children to come over from Europe. Host families are recruited whom the children board with. I am sure that there are more of these schools than we are aware of. As the children stay less than 28 days there is no requirement for local authorities to be informed. These situations remain unregulated.

We also deal with a guardianship organisation which recruits host families for children from independent schools. We undertake social services checks on the families.

Children from Belorussia stay with host families as part of a holiday scheme organised by the local branch of a national organisation. They contacted the department and we agreed to undertake safeguard checks on the host families. There are other groups that take children from abroad, often featured in articles in the local press about fundraising, and we need to contact them.

We still have a long way to go. We must make parents and carers aware that they have to notify us. We can stick an advert in a paper and think we have done our bit. But promoting awareness is a continuous thing. We have leaflets but we must change their format every now and then and look at the most effective place to put them. My manager has suggested putting a flyer with the salary slips of council employees. We need to approach the local social work training courses. People coming off courses don't seem to have heard of private fostering.

I am not saying that our present structure can deal with the increase in referrals. What is becoming clear is that there are a group of children who can rightly be called children 'in need' as well as a group of vulnerable 15–16 year olds, who are in need of services. For teenagers who have left home and their parents, there is a need for reconciliation and mediation work. I understand that there are some SSDs which say they have no privately fostered children. But if they looked for them, they would find them.

In child minding, once the concept of registration came in, standards improved. The same would happen if private foster carers had to be registered. Registration would offer a status and approval which our present system of just accepting private carers does not. It would also raise awareness amongst fieldwork teams and the public.

If you accept the estimates in the Utting Report then there are more children in private foster homes than in children's homes. It is only a matter of time before something serious happens in a private fostering situation.

I have come across private foster carers who have taken in a difficult child who otherwise would have been accommodated by the local authority. They have proved good carers and they don't want money. There are good people. On the other hand, I have been aware of situations where arrangements are breaking down and we need to work with them to improve the situation, or to look for an alternative arrangement. It is important that such cases have a social worker allocated and to see that children are not denied access to services because they are privately fostered.

Marcia Spencer

Marcia Spencer was born in Jamaica. Until recently she was black issues project manager with the British Agencies for Adoption and Fostering, and its joint facilitator of the Private Fostering Practice Issues Group.

I came to this country from Jamaica at the age of five to join my parents. I had lived in Jamaica with my mum's sister. We lived in Stockwell and had a fairly big house and, when my mum was between jobs, she started child minding. Some of these children stayed overnight and were what we would now call privately fostered. She was the kind of person to whom people turned for advice and soon we had a number of children, some stayed for years and their parents visited. I am the only child so it was a part of my life to have other children around. They were mostly Caribbean. I was generally older than them so I was very involved in the care of them. My dad loved young children but he was not very involved in the day to day care being out at work. So private fostering has been in my family for a long time.

My parents also let out some of our rooms, just to make ends meet. It was hard for black people in those days. They couldn't get loans so we always had a number of Nigerian families in the house. The so-called divide between Africans and Caribbeans is not my experience.

I went to a secondary modern school and then to the University of Essex to do sociology. When I finished my degree, I wrote to Lambeth SSD and went to work as a residential social worker in Lambeth's complex of children's homes near Croydon. I wasn't that much older than some of the young people I was caring for. The numbers of black children in this very white setting seemed to stand out. I was then lucky to be seconded for social work training, came back to residential care and then moved to the fostering and adoption unit and that is where I became professionally interested in private fostering.

The unit had two white, middle aged women, Jeanne MacLean and Sheila Calder, who had set up a system whereby West African parents, mainly students, came in to see them and they would try to identify private fostering families whom they approved in the borough. I was very interested and sat in on some of their interviews. Jean and Sheila were white, married, older, and the West Africans who came in were very respectful to them. The advice they gave, and this was before the 1989 Children Act, about keeping contact with their children was accepted. Unfortunately that system does not operate any more. All this time, I was also doing the fostering and adoption work, as well. What I liked about Lambeth was that, as a practitioner, you had a lot of opportunity to develop. If you had an idea, you could run with it. Most local authorities are very different now and it is difficult to be creative.

I left Lambeth in 1987 when I came to BAAF as the black issues trainer and consultant. I continued my interest in private fostering and the Private Fostering Practice Issues Group evolved in the late 1980s and early 1990s. We failed to get funding from the Department of Health for this. But one thing we could do was to bring people together for a private fostering forum. My personal objective was to try and keep private fostering on the agenda of BAAF. I was also very concerned about the placement outcomes of private foster children. At that time, I saw private fostering as mostly about West African children in white families so my motivation was also how we could help the children and the families in their situations. I had the Lambeth model in my mind and I knew that it could work if the input was there.

I contributed to a publication by the Race Equality Unit, *Black Children and Private Fostering*, in 1993. It raised the issue of trans-racial placements. In the introduction there was a letter from a black mother who had placed her child and then lost her after a battle in the courts. The book showed some of the dangers for the birth parents. BAAF published a number of helpful pamphlets. One was for birth parents and another particularly valuable one gave advice to private foster carers. I also went to a conference in Nigeria about private fostering set up by the African Fostering Advisory Service with the Nigerian government.

My colleague Peter Wrighton and myself have kept the Private Fostering Group going and it is now recognised as a reference group and the Department of Health are represented on it. It has been a networking opportunity for new social workers. There is still a pattern whereby new social workers, or students, get given this area of work but, over the last few years, more interest has come from senior practitioners and managers and the group provides an opportunity for them to come together to share policy and practice plans. It highlights the trans-racial element in private fostering. We have not been able to do as much lobbying of government as we would have liked. However, in terms of the Utting Report we have been very clear that the recommendations about private fostering should be implemented.

It was a disappointment that the proposal for the registration of private foster carers was not implemented. There is a strong view that private fostering is a private arrangement and should not be over-regulated. But the government makes pronouncements about other private matters. I don't know whether it is that private fostering is seen as primarily affecting black children and families which explains why the government is not wanting really to touch it. For me, this is tied to institutional racism. Also there is now the view that the system is being abused by people who don't have permission to be in this country. But many birth parents are highly motivated people who are studying and working hard and who need support in finding good care for their children.

My main concern now is getting the registration of foster carers implemented. Next we must make sure that trans-racial issues are not lost if there is to be more focus on other types of private fosterings such as teenagers and overseas students. We must be aware of the sexual and emotional abuse that can occur within private foster homes.

The government is to promote an awareness campaign about private fostering. This is important but I do not think the plans for the present one are on a big enough scale. It needs to be on TV so that the messages are directly communicated. The approach is too passive, not proactive enough. The government could do much more to challenge local authorities than they do now. For example, why wasn't private fostering a part of Quality Protects which set targets and standards for SSDs in so many child care matters? It is concerned about the number of moves of looked after children and stipulates that no child should move more than three times in one year. But private foster children can be moved every other week and nothing is said. The educational support to children in care is now regarded as very important but what about the support for private foster children? Private fostering is viewed negatively and unless and until proper safeguards are in place, this will remain the case. West African children, in my view, remain one of the most vulnerable groups with much to lose if the system remains the same.

Dr Jenny Taylor and Dr Melissa Cook

Dr Jenny Taylor is a clinical psychologist and project leader of the children looked after mental health services, Lambeth. Dr Melissa Cook is a clinical psychologist at the children looked after mental health services, Lambeth.

Dr Taylor
The first time I ever heard the term private fostering was in 1998 when a boy of seven was referred to me when I was working for a general practitioner practice. I did not know what it was and it had not come into my training.

The only private foster children I now see are ones with problems. There may be many others who do not display problems. I'll talk about one case in my present post. Initially it was referred by a GP who stated that an eight year old West African boy was being bullied at school. The problem seemed to be with his peers. He was living with his mother and two younger siblings. The mother had gone to the GP concerned about his behaviour at school and home but mainly at school.

I met with the mother and found out that she had a partner with whom she had difficulties. She explained that the boy had been privately fostered with white carers in the West Country from the age of one and a half to six. So his first memories were all of being in a white family in a predominantly white area. He had been back with his mum for about two and a half years when I got involved. The boy constantly asked to see his private foster parents which upset and annoyed the mother. To her, it was not that big a deal, she had simply made a child care arrangement. She told him that the foster carers did not want to see him any more. But what she explained to me, and what one of the carers told me, was that they found it very upsetting to see him because they had had him for so long but they did not label this as a rejection. The way the mum explained it to the boy, he interpreted it as a rejection. She thought that a clean break was the easiest way to do it. But she did not understand the impact this was having on the boy.

We did quite a bit of work around drawings of families. When I asked him to draw his previous foster family, he labelled them as 'my brother', 'my sister', he did not say 'my foster brother', 'my foster sister'. I tried to get the mother and the boy to discuss together the different families they had had. Initially her attitude was that it just made it worse to talk about it. I felt strongly that the little boy had things he did not understand and that needed to be heard. I did not think it helpful for me to see him individually but that it was important for his mum to create space to discuss these matters with him. We did a lot of drawing and talking in which he remembered his friends in the previous placement and talked about why he moved from one place to another. He was also the only child in the family who was previously fostered. There were younger siblings but she had kept them with her. So that was a major question for him, why had he been sent away and the others hadn't?

We did create a life story book and I remember seeing his little face light up when he talked about when he was originally with mum in Nigeria. I got her to bring in pictures about it. I saw more animation than ever before as he saw photos of himself. Mum had been concerned about stirring up the past but I encouraged them to share the narrative. She told him anecdotes about himself as a baby in Nigeria and he learned that he did have a history.

Sadly it was quite difficult to do very much because she was in the context of a difficult relationship which meant that this was one of her least priorities. This was also a reason why it was such a problem for the child. If he had returned to a family that was more contained, it might not have arisen with such force.

The mother did end up taking an interest in support for herself in the relationship she was in. She was having domestic violence. She also agreed to make time with the boy to work through the life book I had created for him. But she then kept not keeping appointments. We sent her a feedback form and she said that the meetings were quite helpful in regard to having someone to talk to about her boy's attitudes and problems and also on being given advice about organisations which help with domestic violence.

I wrote several letters and phone calls regarding my concerns about the children being left 'home alone' and their mother's need for support, but only got to speak to a social worker once and I did not feel that the family received any substantive social work support.

With regard to private fostering in general, there are a couple of comments. If birth parents are to to use private foster carers then there are difficulties for them in assessing the carers. They can't do police checks. This can only be done effectively by officials. But will private fostering continue if it becomes too regulated? The birth parents want to exercise responsibility while the carers do not want too many visits and regulations. A balance has to be reached.

The other thing is that people trying to place their children in foster homes should have some kind of psychological input to help them. They need to know what difficulties are likely to arise in the future, what the trans-racial issues are and how children can be brought back from private foster homes.

Dr Cook

The first case I took here was a boy who had been privately fostered. I had never heard of it. We held a professionals' meeting with the social worker and were joined by a cultural interpreter who advised us on private fostering.

The boy was 11years, black and of Nigerian heritage. The referral stated that he had been in private foster care since birth and his mum had removed him from the foster home to home and since then he had been running away. On occasions he had been returned by the police. He had problems of identity and thought of himself as white. At the meeting, we found out that he had been fostered from eight weeks old. The foster carers were white British in Havant and his younger sister also went there. The boy had had little contact with his birth mother and father. There was an incident when dad went down in 1995 to take the children but that lasted only a couple of weeks and they were returned.

In 2000, the mum decided to take the children back and had gone to the private foster carers' house to take them. The police were called and it was traumatic for all. Later they did move back to London with the parents. The boy kept absconding from home and from school where he was bullied. He was subsequently taken into care and placed with another foster home in Lambeth. The SSD wanted our involvement and it was decided that the cultural interpreter would work with the birth mother to bring her to the point where she would be able to meet with myself to do some family work about rehabilitating the boy to his home.

Before I got to see them, the foster carer phoned to say that the birth mother had removed the child and taken him to Nigeria against his wishes. He still wanted to go back to his previous foster carers. I was very concerned about how this was going to affect his mental health and I was not sure what kind of power we had in this country to bring him back. I contacted the child protection adviser and he said that there was not a lot we could do as the mother had parental responsibility.

Part 3
Private Fostering Today and Tomorrow

Chapter 9: Private Fostering at Present

Private fostering is still largely unknown even amongst welfare professionals. Two highly qualified clinical psychologists, who were interviewed for the last chapter, heard nothing about it in their training. Yet, although so unknown, various pieces of legislation about private fostering have come on to the statute book in the last 50 years. To clarify matters, this chapter will start by drawing upon the Department of Health's most recent leaflet which summarises the legal definition and duties about private fostering.

The leaflet *Private Fostering: A Cause for Concern* states that private fostering 'occurs when a child under 16 (if disabled under 18) is cared for, for more than 28 days by an adult who is not a relative, by private arrangement between parent and carer'. It continues that private foster carers must 'advise their local council of their intention to foster a child at least six weeks in advance or, where an emergency placement is made, within 48 hours of the child's arrival'. Further, they must 'notify their local council when a child leaves their care, stating why and giving the name and address of the person into whose care the child has been moved'.

The duties of the local council are to 'check on the suitability of private foster carers', to 'make regular visits to the child', to 'ensure that advice is made available when needed' and to 'observe the overall standard of care' (Department of Health, 2001).

Knowledge about private fostering is very limited compared with the many studies of fosterings arranged by local authorities. Yet interviews with former private foster children, private foster carers, and professionals who specialise in it, taken in conjunction with a handful of small studies and my own experience, do enable some conclusions to be drawn. This final part of the book will therefore deal with the state of private fostering at present, the current involvement of local authorities with it, and the present policies of central government. The findings will lead to proposals for good social work practice and for more enlightened legislation.

How Many Private Foster Children?

During the early 1990s, the government recorded numbers of notified private foster children had fallen to around 2,000. Some SSDs and SWDs declared that they had few if any private foster children. The impression was created that private fostering was in decline and the government stopped collecting the statistics.

However, the fact that the number of *notified* private foster children was small did not necessarily mean that the actual number had declined. It can mean that private foster carers were not giving notice of them and/or that social workers were not looking for them. Beverley Clarke conducted a small local investigation amongst welfare professionals and estimated that the area contained about a hundred private foster children, most of whom were not notified (Rickford, 1995). In Gloucestershire, Brendan McGrath has adopted a pro-active approach and during the year 2000 received 78 private fostering referrals. As he said in the interview, 'I understand that there are some SSDs which say that they have no private foster children. But if they looked for them they would find them.' The very experienced Angus Geddes reckoned in 2001 that the city where he worked had 20–30 private foster children although hardly any had been notified. Plymouth is a city which is known to have received an influx of West African private foster children. Yet very few are known to the SSD and its family placement officer concedes, 'We don't know how many are out there. And even if we knew about them, we have limited resources we could devote to helping them' (Cited by Traynor, 2001). Somewhat belatedly, the Department of Health now concedes that probably the number of private foster children is around 10,000 (Department of Health, 2001). Interestingly, the number of children in local authority, voluntary and private residential establishments in 2000 was 1,146. These children quite rightly receive much attention and resources from welfare bodies. Yet private foster children, whose numbers make them one of the largest groups of vulnerable children in Britain, receive little consideration from official agencies.

Satisfactory Private Foster Carers

It does no service to portray all private foster carers as unsatisfactory or dangerous. Those SSDs which do assess private carers appear to grade most as satisfactory: although this is not to say they would accept them to be local authority foster carers.

Former foster child Christine Hanks declared, 'It is through private fostering that I met this woman, she's like an angel. Had that not happened I would not be the person I am today. I am very proud to be her daughter'. This is not to say that Christine faced no difficulties and, in adulthood, she was still dealing with her anger towards her natural parents. It is to say that she enjoyed a warm and secure upbringing.

Yvonne Martins, who was fostered from the age of six months, also spoke positively about her private carer, saying, 'I can remember being loved a lot by my foster mother'. Somewhat against her will, at the age of eight Yvonne was taken back by her parents and went to Nigeria. Yet when she returned to Britain as an adult, she lived with her foster carer.

Interestingly, Sylvia Ackfield and Roland Webb were in the same foster home but developed different perceptions of their foster mother. Sylvia disliked her sharp temper and her reluctance to show affection. Simultaneously, she appreciated how the foster mother encouraged her education and her genuine concern. Sylvia's ambivalence was shown when she left, for she stated, 'I suppose I loved her because I looked upon her as my mother. The strange part is that I don't remember feeling sad when I left'.

Roland Webb also commented that 'there wasn't any closeness or affection' and left as soon as he could. However, he maintained contact with his private foster mother and said, 'The good thing was that I was in one place for my childhood. It wasn't maybe a happy place but it was one place. We didn't have any kind of abuse. We were not hit or beaten'.

Turning to the interviews with the private foster carers, Mr and Mrs Cahalin are of interest for two reasons. One is that they had also fostered for a local authority. The other was that the foster father played a major part in the fosterings which previous research has shown to be unusual (Holman, 1973, p87–103). The Cahalins appeared to have turned to private fostering because the local authority placed older rather than younger children with them. They soon found that their services were in demand from natural parents.

In like manner, Mrs Johnson had the trust of a number of West African parents. Here standards of care appeared to have pleased the visiting social workers while the one child whom she had kept into teenager years was doing well at school. Mrs Johnson appreciated that West African children required special skin and hair care and had encouraged her teenager to visit Ghana. In contrast to the Cahalins, her husband objected to black children and she regarded this difference as one of the factors which led to their divorce.

The Cahalins and Mrs Johnson were really professional foster carers who looked after a series of children. By contrast, others found themselves in situations where they took in just one child. Mrs Helen Mitchell took in a niece. Close relatives are not usually classed as private foster children, although the local authority deemed her to be one. The arrangement was obviously successful with Mrs Mitchell concluding, 'We gave her a lot of love but anything we ever did for her we've had back tenfold ... Not a day goes by when she does not phone.' Miss Pauline Hawkins took on the daughter of her partner after he left.

Despite the girl's unstable background, she settled, wanted to stay and persuaded social workers to let her do so. Ms Clare Bryan's own background of instability and drugs would probably counted against her had she applied to foster for the local authority. Yet Rena, also from a deprived background, seemed to choose her as her foster mother and after five years had clearly made progress. Rena said of her foster carer, 'She brings me up well . . . I can talk with her'.

Two of the private foster carers acknowledged that their foster children had been too much for them. Mrs Marlene Box had agreed with her daughter's request to give accommodation to her 15 year old friend who had been thrown out of her own home. The girl had severe problems, truanted, was anorexic and physically harmed herself. Her presence disrupted the family but it only ended when the teenager ran away with a man. In like manner, Mrs Betty Sutton took in one of the friends of her teenage son. Despite receiving little financial support from his father, she persevered with the boy until his adverse influence on her own children brought about the end of the fostering. She still had some regrets saying, 'I do have feelings for him: I took him into my own home' and she continued to have some contact with him.

Both these private foster mothers were motivated to help. Both displayed some capacities to communicate with deprived young persons. And both felt that they might have coped if they had received closer and more skilled support from social workers.

28 years ago, I published the first major study of private fostering. From a large sample and a number of forms of assessment, I concluded that 45 per cent of the private foster parents were suitable while 55 per cent possessed at least one unsuitability factor: which did not necessarily mean they should not foster but did put a question mark over them (Holman, 1973, chapter 4). My impression from this review and from the interviews is that matters have not changed substantially. The suitable ones are of three kinds:

1. Very capable foster carers who provide affection, stability, firm but kind discipline and who have insights into the needs of their private foster children.
2. Adequate carers whose physical standards are beyond reproach but whose parenting strengths are impaired by certain deficiencies. They may be caring but somewhat distant. They may be affectionate but with limited understanding of children's cultural and ethnic needs, warm and protective but unwilling to encourage constant contact with the natural parents.
3. Highly motivated foster carers. Often those who may have succeeded in bringing up their own children and feel they have the abilities to take on youngsters whose behaviour, demands and needs then prove too much for them. These private foster mothers particularly need the guidance and support from social workers who have expertise in child care.

Unprepared, Unsatisfactory and Unsafe Private Foster Carers

The positive nature of some private foster carers should not be used to hide the unsatisfactory nature of others. Numbers undertake fostering without appreciating that children should not be moved from one home to another without careful preparation and planning. Mary Tapper, as a seven year old in Sierra Leone, found herself 'in a totally strange environment' when her parents placed her with a teacher. By the age of ten, she was in Britain where, without warning, the teacher put her in a private foster home in Kent. Mary never saw her parents or the teacher again. The interviews reveal that children were put with foster parents they had never seen before, without any understanding of what was happening to them, and without the foster carers collecting basic information about their diet, health and habits.

Once in a private foster home, children may be moved on elsewhere. Kriss Akabusi has vague memories of several foster homes. Sometimes the abrupt move may be back to their own parents. Private foster carer Mrs Cahalin told of natural parents who 'came unexpectedly, they took the children and we never saw them again. But another parent told me how upset one of the children was at being pulled away from us'. Yvonne Martins, aged eight, went back to her parents with no preparation. She commented, 'I cried, I couldn't believe it. I kept on looking at the faces of people who I thought could be my foster mother when I was out or going to school'. In my original study, I demonstrated that many private foster children were not prepared adequately for traumatic changes of homes (Holman, 1973, chapter 5). Nearly 30 years later, many are still likely to experience the same pain, distress, and trauma of sudden changes.

Prepared or unprepared, some private foster children go to carers who are just not suitable for the fostering role. Kriss Akabusi and his brother were put with an elderly woman so ill that she spent most of the time in bed. Reports were heard of private foster carers whose own children had been in public care, who were blatantly racially prejudiced, who took in as many as five children at one time, who never displayed affection or warmth, who kept their foster children isolated from the community and who refused to co-operate with officials.

Worst of all, some private foster children were emotionally, physically and sexually abused. Margaret McMinn was constantly told that her mother was a 'guttersnipe'. She had little recreation, had to work on the farm and was 'leathered with the tube from the milking machine'. She broke down in the interview but she may well have been sexually abused as well. Kriss Akabusi and his brother went to one foster home which was cruel by Dickensian standards. Kriss was made to drink his own urine. The boys were beaten with a belt and a slipper. They were unloved and unwanted. Mary Tapper explained, 'A few weeks later, my foster father started to sexually abuse me. I was 11. You get yourself into a kind of mood where it's not you it's happening to. I remember thinking that if he was doing it to me then he's not going to do it with the younger ones. But he was abusing them as well'.

Key Issues

This study has looked at contemporary articles about private fostering and listened to those who participate in it. From all sources, two key issues emerge.

The first concerns the difficulties faced by black children who are placed with white foster carers. Kriss Akabusi recalled that, even as a young child, he knew he was different because other children pointed out that he had 'very small ears, large lips and a broad nose.' But it was years before he felt able to explore his African background and went to Nigeria.

Iris Grant, in her interview, revealed that, from the age of 14 to 18, she never spoke to another black person. She said, 'It was obvious that the other people did not want me mixing with their children. All the school children were invited to one another's parties and I was always excluded'. She appreciated her loving foster parents but felt that they ignored her blackness. She continued '. . . how much better it would have been if they had acknowledged my blackness and given me some books and magazines which took into account that I am black or talked about the problems I would have to face'.

Christine Hanks said of her fostering environment, 'In Kent it was a white area and I was about the only black person in the school and I got bullied a lot'. She was close to her white foster mother but, as Christine explained, 'She didn't know what to do. It was not that she could not be bothered, she just didn't know what to tell us to do'. She added, 'There is no support or training for foster carers in dealing with black children'. In like manner, Christine considered that insufficient attention was given to her roots and culture. Today she does not feel the same as African people because she cannot cook or do her hair as they do. Her foster carer did not understand how to help her in the face of racism.

Yvonne Martins was also happy with her white foster mother but, when she met teasing and name calling at school, she too felt that her foster mother was not aware of her need for help. Then, when she was abruptly returned to her black parents, she met difficulties in moving back into the culture and language in which she had been born but which she had forgotten.

Mary Tapper was told by her foster mother that she did not want any black faces in the home. She recorded, 'I can remember thinking if only I could just shrink or disappear'. She also met difficulties as a black pupil in a predominantly white school. The fact that her basic language was not English and that she had been traumatised by her moves was not appreciated by teachers who put her in a special needs class. Mary did eventually succeed academically but she never succeeded in regaining her culture. She commented sadly, 'I have lost my culture. I am neither African nor western'.

Welfare professionals made similar observations. Private fostering specialist, Heather Clacy commented that a couple of elderly white carers did relate well with their black private foster child but they were unable to help her sort out her identity, to give her knowledge of her culture, and to enable her to cope with racial tauntings. She concluded, 'It is the cultural side which worries me most, the lack of contact private foster children have with children from a similar cultural background . . . (they) are going to lose their language and much more'.

Beverley Clarke, who has seen many black private foster children, noticed, 'These children are trans-racially placed in areas where there are few or no black people like themselves. So there are no black role models for them. When they return home, they have difficulties relating to their black parents. They lack insight and knowledge about their culture and identity. There is confusion as they get older and realise they are different. They are left in emotional turmoil'.

The clinical psychologists Dr Jenny Taylor and Dr Melissa Cook had both taken on children whose behavioural difficulties stemmed from being black children in white foster homes. Dr Cook had a boy who, having been with white foster carers almost from birth, was taken back by his black mother when he was 11. He continued to think of himself as white and ran away from home. Probably against his wishes, the mother took him to Nigeria.

It is not denied that some white foster carers can be sensitive to and skilled in bringing up children whose racial roots and cultural backgrounds are different from their own. But the evidence is that such trans-racial placements often hinder children who have already gone through the emotional trauma of separation from their birth parents. The main difficulties are as follows:

- It is a shock for black children who move from a black upbringing to a white family and neighbourhood whose habits, values, behaviour, background and even language are so different from that they have experienced.
- Racist taunts and verbal abuse from school children and, in some cases, even from foster carers. They are not necessarily spoken abuse. Iris Grant suffered when she was shunned by others, when she was excluded from the activities of her school mates.
- Education difficulties. Black children placed in predominantly white schools may be perceived as backward or naughty because their language and behaviour is different from others and because the emotional stresses they are facing within their foster homes are making them withdrawn. Consequently, they do not receive the same stimulation and encouragement as other children of their age.
- The children feel baffled, hurt and powerless when their foster carers do not perceive the problems of racism they are experiencing or do not know how to help the children deal with them.
- Those children who, at a later stage, do return to their black parents then find this a painful process as they must adapt to behaviour, talk, food, habits, with which they have grown unfamiliar.

- The loss of culture. It seems that many black private foster children are not given access to learn about and to understand the cultures from which they originated. As they reach adulthood, they may feel alienated from their own culture. Iris Grant, born in Africa and raised in a white foster home revealed, 'I always feel uncomfortable with black people. Even now I don't have black friends. I am comfortable with white people . . . I would say that I am just a little English girl under a black skin'. Other former private foster children felt that they could identify with neither white nor black cultures.
- Associated with a loss of culture is bewilderment about identity. Christine Hanks and Iris Grant, on the surface, had satisfying childhoods and success in careers. Yet because, while in their foster homes, they had little contact with black people, they later had some difficulties in relating with them.

The second key issue concerns the amount of contact between the private foster children and their natural parents and other family members. No doubt some natural parents do visit their children frequently and regularly. Mrs Johnson, who took many foster children, encouraged visits (except in the first month). But the indicators are that many parents do not maintain close contact. Mr and Mrs Cahalin were not adverse to parents visiting but, perhaps because numbers lived long distances away, it was not unusual for them to call only every four to six months. It is the long term private foster children who seem most likely to have little contact. The parents of Sylvia Ackfield came only occasionally. Kriss Akabusi's parents went back to Nigeria. Iris Grant did not see hers after the age of 14. Rena Rogers observed, 'I don't see my mum much now'. Christine Hanks had little contact with her family while Mary Tapper was never visited at all.

There are instances where it is in the children's interests not to see abusive and dangerous parents. But, as I showed years ago, usually regular contact helps them settle in their foster homes and makes it easier for them to eventually return home. Not least, when regular contact is maintained there is less chance of foster carers deciding, understandably, that they want to keep the children permanently even when the natural parents do not want this. Experience shows that foster carers are less likely to come to this decision if the natural family keeps in the picture while courts are much more likely to make custody orders or residence orders in favour of the carers where there has been little contact (Holman, 1973, p186–8). No doubt this is why the Guidance and Regulations advise natural parents and private foster parents 'on the importance of continuing links for the children's emotional welfare' (Department of Health, 1991, para. 1.4.34).

The interviews with the former private foster children well illustrate why contact is important. For a start, separated children do tend to have a need to understand their past. Their own identity is bound up with who their parents were and their pain at being apart from them may be assuaged if they know why their parents parted with them. Margaret McMinn, as a young woman, felt impelled to trace her mother and father. Neither fully welcomed her but at least she met them and gained some insights into why they had not looked after her. Roland Webb was frustrated when his foster mother rebuffed all his queries about his parents. He has spent much of his adulthood seeking answers and feels he can not be fully at peace until he knows all there is to know. Margaret and Roland would have been spared much pain and trouble if they had seen their parents regularly as children.

Next, black children are more likely to lose their culture and identity if they do not see their families. Iris Grant and Christine Hanks, for instance, would have understood their backgrounds, could have related to black people, could have felt a part of a family if their parents and relatives had been a part of their lives. And children like Yvonne Martins could have experienced a less painful return home if she had not almost lost touch with her family.

Not least, regular visits can prevent abuse. If Margaret McMinn's parents and Mary Tapper's 'mother' had called on them only once a month, they would have presented the opportunity for the children to reveal what was happening.

The Effects of Private Fostering

Mention has already been made of the long term effects on black children of being raised with white carers where they had little contact with black people. How does private fostering affect children more generally? Of course, it is impossible to be precise. Their characters and personalities are shaped by a multitude of factors including genetics and their experiences before they went to the private foster homes. None the less, it is valuable to record what the participants said.

Mrs Helen Mitchell was pleased that her foster child became a well-adjusted person, successful in her occupation and a happy wife and parent. Yvonne Martins was thankful that her private foster mother introduced her to Christianity which has stayed with her into adulthood. She is now a social worker and commented on her childhood, 'I believe it has made me a better social worker because I have gone through the experience of separation and loss myself. So when I am relating with young people I can empathise with them'.

Christine Hanks made a mixed assessment. She stated that her loving foster mother gave her a good emotional grounding so that she has become a stable, well-educated young woman. But she also feels that fostering cut her off from her own family while, being black, she can never be fully a part of her foster family. The outcome, she says is that 'I do not feel I have a close family structure'. She continued, 'I feel anger towards my parents, my mother more than my dad ... she doesn't show any remorse for what they did to us'. Recently, Christine went to counselling in order to help with her deep anger. Iris Grant said, 'As a result of being fostered, I would say that I am a very mixed-up person. It did not hit me until I was in my thirties. I have a lot of superficial friendships just as I did as a foster child. People could only like me for a certain period of the day. I am now having counselling to deal with my past. I haven't made deep relationships'. She added, 'I've a lot of anger, bitterness and sadness about what has happened to me both by my natural parents and foster parents . . . I have this void in my life that I don't belong anywhere. I have no family'.

Kriss Akabusi believes that his 'experiences away from my parents gave me an intense need to be accepted and recognised. Out of this has come my intense desire to achieve'. Oddly enough, Kriss's childhood deprivations may have cultivated the motivation which led to him winning gold medals for athletics. But, he adds, 'In the personal relationships I am not so happy. We were moved so many times, my memory is of being torn from people I had become fond of. I learned never to let myself feel secure or that this was really home. Because I never learned how to give and receive in a natural way, I found it difficult in later life to be spontaneously loving with those closest to me . . . I have few really close friends. Even with my wife, whom I love very much, I hold something back. I learned that trusting people led to pain'.

Margaret McMinn was constantly told by her foster mother that her natural mother was dirty with the implication that her faults would somehow be transmitted to Margaret. She spoke of her 'fear that this terrible dirt is in me. That it is still with me and I now clean things unnecessarily because I fear that things will get dirty. I have to see that things are straight. I can't leave it. I used to think that if I scrubbed myself clean my 'mother' would love me'. She told about her difficulties in relating with other adults and added, 'If someone in the church says something, I can feel so rejected. I see a lot of mistakes in the way I've brought up my children. With my eldest, I would only cuddle him when nobody was about. I was following my childhood through again, you go with the pattern'. Margaret underwent some psychiatric treatment and it says much for her resolve, aided by her Christian faith, that she has survived.

Mary Tapper recorded, 'Being fostered has had a profound effect on me. It made me not trust. I lost confidence in my own judgement. Even when I know what I am doing is right, I am never 100 per cent sure'. She added that her sister, who was in the same foster home, also had 'a lot of psychological problems'.

Roland Webb acknowledged that, 'Some of my life has been a psychological hell . . . I don't really feel a part. As you get older that gets worse'. He reckons that his fostering upbringing has impaired his capacity to trust others and make lasting relationships. He feels that he has been excluded from having a family and from much of what other people have. He noted, 'They (parents) can shut their children out and that's what happened to me'.

It appears that private fostering can sometimes involve children in experiences of separation, loss, trauma, rejection, lack of affection, instability and isolation which not only create immediate childhood distress but which can adversely affect them as adults. Iris Amoah, who as a social worker with the Nigerian High Commission, saw many private fosterings, adds that these adverse effects may also impair their parenting abilities, 'I worked with some parents who had been privately fostered themselves and, as a result, feel unable to address their own needs let alone their children's needs. They had been damaged by being fostered and it is heart-breaking to see them feeling isolated and not knowing where to go'.

Other children, as well as private foster children, are separated from their families. No doubt those looked after by SSDs and SWDs with local authority foster carers and in residential establishments are also affected by being away from their parents. But, at least, they are likely to have regular contact with social services staff who can offer professional help. The next question concerns the extent to which local authorities provide a service for private foster children, their parents and carers.

Local Authorities and Private Fostering

As explained in earlier chapters, a series of statutes have placed duties in regard to private fostering upon local authorities. The most recent are, for England and Wales, the Children Act (1989) in conjunction with the Guidance and Regulations and in Scotland The Foster Children (Scotland) Act (1984) followed by regulations and the Children (Scotland) Act (1995). How have local authorities fulfilled their duties and pursued good practice towards private foster children, private foster carers and the natural parents?

Local authorities have a duty to satisfy themselves that '*the welfare of private foster children is safeguarded*'. Before children go to the private foster home, they are empowered to order disqualified persons not to take children and can prohibit other persons, or their premises, if they are unsuitable. But preventing children going to such homes depends upon the proper working of the notification system whereby private foster carers and natural parents have a duty to notify local authorities of intended placements at least six weeks before they take place. Yet Margaret McMinn and Kriss Akabusi were thrashed in private foster homes which never came to the notice of the authorities. Yvonne Martins was in a foster home for years and then suddenly returned to her parents without any official knowledge. Three social workers in current practice agree that many private fosterings are never reported. Iris Amoah and Angus Geddes, in their interviews, record that they have seen private foster children who are not known to the SSDs. Heather Clacy acknowledged, 'The notification system does not work. I can think of only one private foster carer who lets me know when a child is going to arrive'. The Department of Health estimates around 10,000 private foster children. A survey by the Association of Directors of Social Services, of which more will be said later, found that 47 SSDs in England and Wales recorded an average of seven fostering arrangements (that is 329 in all). If the average is applied nationwide then there would be 1,253 private arrangements which is far below the estimated 10,000 (ADSS, 2001, p3). Not only are most arrangements not notified to the authorities before the children arrive, they are never notified at all. Local authorities have not made the notification system work and hence can not fulfil their duty to safeguard the children.

Obviously, local authorities do, eventually, find out about or receive notifications about some children after they have been in private foster homes. Yet action to prohibit unsuitable private foster carers or to remove children appears rare. The reasons are that to do so would entail the children having yet another change, that the natural parents do not want the fosterings to end, that social workers do not seemed geared up to or experienced in taking such action, and that if the fosterings did come to an end the SSD would be hard-pressed to find an alternative for them.

Local authorities also have a duty *'to advise private foster carers'* about their care of children and, as the Guidance and Regulations indicate can spend money to support them in their tasks. Clearly some social workers do so. Angus Geddes ran support groups for private foster parents, although he had to raise the money for toys and equipment from charities. Yet, after a few years, this work crumbled as his SSD lost interest. Just as clearly some private foster carers are rarely visited. Even when visits are made, the carers might complain that the guidance and support was insufficient. Mrs Marlene Box and Mrs Betty Sutton complained that they were desperate for but never received expert guidance regarding their demanding foster children. The Cahalins commented favourably about their social worker then added, 'But he was for the children who were in care. We informed them when we took private children but he didn't do any checking'. Clare Bryan said that it took three years before the social worker took a positive interest while Pauline Hawkins also went through a period when social workers were 'hostile' towards her before they became more helpful.

Importantly, local authorities have a duty *'to visit the private foster children'*. The Guidance and Regulations stipulate that during the first year of a placement, they should be seen within one week of its commencement and at least every six weeks thereafter. In subsequent years, they should be visited at least every three months. In addition, social workers are told to seek the views of the private foster children and, where appropriate, to see them alone. A few social workers do follow these instructions. Heather Clacy said, 'I visit the children the number of times according to the legal requirement but more often if there are problems. I do see the children on their own and some carers are more co-operative than others about this. I talk with them about what is happening at home, at school. They know that I am making sure that they are all right in the foster home'.

But the former foster children who were interviewed tended to complain about the lack of social work contact. Sylvia Ackfield explained, 'We were given strict instructions not to speak unless they (social workers) spoke to us'. Christine Hanks noted, 'A social worker used to come. Not very often . . . I knew mum wasn't my real mum but I still did not understand why the social worker came. I never saw her alone and she never spoke to me about being black'. Mary

Tapper was desperate to reveal that she was being abused yet, '. . . never once did we get to talk to the social worker without our foster parents there. Before he came, we were told you had better not say anything or you will go back to Africa. It was the time of the Biafran war with terrible pictures on TV. So, of course, I was scared'. In similar vein, Roland Webb wanted to talk about his past, wanted to express his anger towards his mother, yet he never spoke to a social worker alone and so had to bottle up his feelings.

SSDs and SWDs have long been advised to maintain contact between the natural parents and the private foster children. As already pointed out, the Guidance and Regulations issued by the Department of Health made the same point and stated that 'the local authority should explore whether firm arrangements can be made to facilitate contact' and suggested that, in some cases, 'financial assistance could be considered' to do so (Department of Health, 1991, paras. 1.4.34–1.4.37). Clearly, social workers need to be in regular touch with the parents in order to get them to initiate and maintain contacts with the children. Yet the evidence is that few meetings occur. Social worker, Heather Clacy, is well aware of the importance of natural parents yet she said, 'I do not see the natural parents unless they live locally . . . I am not encouraged to make trips to London to see parents'. Local authorities which are unwilling to bear the costs of social workers travelling to see natural parents are unlikely to spend money to facilitate the parents seeing their children.

The State of Private Fostering

The system of private fostering is patchy to say the least. A minority of social workers who do specialise in private fostering, sometimes called dedicated social workers, have tried to make the notification system work, do attempt to safeguard private foster children, do advise and support private foster carers, do want to contact the natural parents. But they are few in number.

To be sure, there are numbers of satisfactory private foster carers. But, generally, the private fostering system is full of holes. The notification system does not work. Almost certainly, hundreds of children are in private foster homes which are unknown to the authorities. Children are moved into private foster homes, between them, and returned to their parents without adequate preparation and planning. Some private foster children are abused and neglected. Some rarely if ever see their parents. Private foster carers, the children and the natural parents receive insufficient visits, advice and counselling. In short, SSDs and SWDs are not delivering the kind of service which legislation instructs them to do. The outcome for the children concerned can be that, as adults, they experience emotional and psychological instability and insecurity.

These conclusions might be challenged on the grounds that the number of interviews was small and that most of the private foster children had experiences that were in the 1960s, 1970s and 1980s rather than from 1990 onwards.

However, the private foster carers and the very experienced professionals who were interviewed were talking about the present. Further, the conclusions were drawn also from a small number of other studies and from my own contacts with the organisations, few as they are, which do take a current interest in private fostering. Perhaps, it is also worth mentioning that I have been concerned with private fostering for nearly 40 years. Children can still be placed in private fosterings which remain unknown to the authorities and with private foster carers who may be unsuitable. If parents do not visit then children have no one to whom they can complain, they are powerless. No wonder that in 1997 Sir William Utting stated that private fostering could be 'a honeypot for abusers' (Department of Health and the Welsh Office, 1997, p45).

Importantly, in 2001, the Association of Directors of Social Services carried out a survey of the involvement of its members with private fostering. Of the 179 social services authorities in England, Wales and Northern Ireland, only 71, that is 41 per cent replied. The fact that the majority had nothing to say is itself an indication of the lack of interest in private fostering. Questionnaires about children looked after by authorities, about child protection, about residential care would get almost 100 per cent replies. Of those that did reply, 49 (69%) indicated that they had drawn up a policy on private fostering while 16 (23%) said they had an officer dedicated to private fostering. If the non-respondents are taken to do little about private fostering, then overall only 27 per cent had a policy and only 9 per cent had a dedicated officer. The probability that all the statutory child care services had just 16 private fostering specialists is a reflection of the claim that private fosterings are neglected by local authorities (ADSS, 2001).

In 1998, Glasgow SWD issued a report on the prioritisation of work within its area teams. Four priorities of children were listed. Private foster children did not rate a mention (Glasgow Social Work Sub Committee, 1998). Amongst SSDs and SWDs, as Heather Clacy said, 'Private fostering is not a priority'. Priority and therefore resources go to children who are in the care of local authorities and those deemed to be in danger within their own homes. Officials sometimes justify this by saying, 'Private fostering is not a statutory responsibility'. Wrong. Extensive legislation exists which shows that local authorities do have statutory responsibilities. By neglecting this responsibility, they neglect some of the most vulnerable children in Britain.

Chapter 10: The Future of Private Fostering

One prime minister, on being asked a question in the Commons about private fostering, promptly answered with reference to children who had been received into the care of local authorities (Holman, 1973, p1). Today few MPs would know much about private fostering. It is not a vote winner and it rarely interests the media. Yet there are compelling reasons why the government should address the issue. The United Nations Convention on the Rights of the Child declares in Article 19, 'The child has a right to protection from abuse and neglect'. Yet, as this study shows, some private foster children are vulnerable to abuse and neglect. Further, if not subjected to these forms of extreme treatment, many private foster children are moved around without preparation and are in homes which do not meet their emotional and cultural needs. Not least, many private foster carers are a valuable resource who need to be supported and helped in order to maximise their parenting capacities for the good of the private foster children. So what can be done to improve private fostering?

The Awareness Campaign

Obviously private foster children can not be helped until all are notified to local authorities. The Department of Health must therefore take some credit for initiating a public awareness campaign and for announcing that its inspectors would examine the private fostering arrangements of some local authorities. Both initiatives did not get off the ground until 2001 and, disappointingly, are proving to be low key. The awareness campaign is limited to one leaflet aimed at informing welfare professionals of the existence of private fostering. Even this is confined to England with no provision made for Wales and Scotland. It would seem even more important to inform the general public about private fostering but officials at the Department of Health say this must wait until a future date. What should the government do? My suggestions are that:

- The private fostering regulations be printed on the back of child benefit books: all parents get child benefit.
- The private fostering regulations should appear on the video machines which play to queues in the post office: we all go to the post office.

- Information about private fostering should go out on advertisements at peak TV hours: perhaps with Kriss Akabusi presenting them.

One can almost hear the government muttering about costs. In fact, the costs are probably less than that of a couple of inquiries into the deaths of abused children.

It is not just the public which needs to become aware of private fostering. Many local authorities need to be more aware of their statutory obligations. One outcome of the Department of Health's inspections of SSDs and SWDs will be to focus their attention on the subject. But, to date, the inspections have been to just five local authorities with supplementary activity in five others. The aim should now be to increase the number of inspections so that within five years all local authorities will have been inspected and so prodded into private fostering action. If one of the inspected items is the extent to which SSDs and SWDs are running local awareness campaigns (perhaps pointing them to Brendan McGrath's activities in Gloucestershire as an example), then between them central and local government should have spread information about private fostering far and wide. Almost certainly, the numbers of known private foster children will increase.

SSDs and SWDs will only take private fostering more seriously when they accept that the needs of private foster children are as great as those looked after by local authorities. In order to ensure this end, the government should pay heed to the proposal put forward by Marcia Spencer in her interview. At present, the government's Quality Protects programme sets targets for local authorities in regard to looked after children. These include, for instance, a reduction in the number of moves experienced by the children and improvements in their educational improvement. Marcia argues that private foster children should be included in the programme. Social workers might then, for example, be given targets to ensure that private foster children have regular health checks, be kept in contact with their siblings and, with reference to black children, that they have their cultural and racial needs taken fully into account. The Department of Health has allocated £885 million over five years to enable local authorities to reach their targets. It is not too much that a million a year be allocated for private fostering targets.

The Local Authority Framework for Private Fostering

The Children Act (1989) and other legislation does place on local authorities duties and powers to deal with private fostering. Unfortunately, as the results of the ADSS survey show, most do not take their responsibilities seriously. The indications are that these SSDs and SWDs do not seek out private foster children. If a notification does come in, there is no established system for assessing the carers and it is likely to be placed on the desk of a social worker who gives it low priority. By contrast, there are a minority of authorities who have set up systems for dealing with private fosterings. The aim must be that all establish such systems, for, without such a framework, private foster children will slip through the departmental holes.

The basic step for any SSD and SWD to take is to compile a *private fostering policy statement*. Such statements outline the private fostering legislation, indicate the department's system for assessing private foster carers and visiting private foster children, discuss the ways in which the children can best be helped and state a commitment towards them. This policy is then put in the hands of all chief officers, all elected members and all social workers. It may be that a private fostering sub-committee of councillors can be established which reports regularly to the main social services or social work committee in order to ensure that the interests of private foster children are kept to the fore.

Within the private fostering framework, an important decision concerns the nature and location of *the staff to be responsible for private fosterings*. Within the departments which do take the matter seriously, three different approaches can be discerned:

1. Some leave private fosterings completely in the hands of area teams where they are allocated to individual field workers who fit them in with all their other child care duties. With new referrals, the social worker would make an assessment which then goes to the area team social work leader for acceptance or not.
2. Others have a dedicated or specialist private fostering officer, often located within a central fostering and adoption unit, who takes all the private foster referrals for a large territory and whose assessments may go to the unit's adoption and fostering panel for acceptance. If not approved, the specialist officer takes steps to bring the placement to a close. If accepted, the foster carers and child are then allocated to the appropriate area team where it goes to a field social worker for visits.
3. The third approach is for the specialist officer not only to report to the adoption and fostering panel but thereafter to keep the case and undertake the visits.

The advantage of the first approach, which can be called the area approach, is that it locates private fostering within an area setting where the social worker should know the neighbourhood in which the child is put. Further, if the fostering breaks down and it becomes a child protection case, then it is already within the team which deals with such cases. The disadvantage is that, because private foster cases are small compared with other child care referrals, individual area social workers will not develop private fostering expertise. Moreover, it seems that hard pressed social workers dealing with children looked after by local authorities are likely to put private fostering at the bottom of the pile. And the prospects of them conducting local awareness campaigns, running groups for private foster parents, seeking out language school placements and so on, seem low. Noticeably, Angus Geddes, in his interview, recorded that after his specialist private foster role was stopped, 'the private fostering cases were redistributed amongst all the social workers and interest declined.'

The second approach, the mixed approach, means that a dedicated or specialist officer concentrates on and develops skills in making assessments of private foster carers once they are notified. Once accepted, the case goes to the area team with the advantages mentioned above. In practice the passage may not be so smooth. One of the experienced professionals who was interviewed mentioned that overburdened area teams may be reluctant to accept new cases from the adoption and fostering panel. In some instances, private fosterings have got stuck between the two. He also pointed out that the reluctance was also partly because the area team did not want another child who would eat into its limited budget.

The third approach, which I call the specialism with continuity approach, has the obvious drawback that the private foster children would be separated from area teams. The disadvantage may not be that great for a specialist private fostering social worker should be appointed only after previous experience and so should be equipped to co-operate with or to hand over to the area team a child who requires wider child care help. My preference is for this approach for these reasons. First, a worker who concentrates just on private fostering would build up the expertise to deal with what is a complex area of fostering. Second, by dealing with referrals, assessments, visits, rehabilitation back to parents and even after-care, this approach would provide a continuity which is lacking if private fosterings are split between them and area teams. Third, having no other child care responsibilities, the private fostering social worker would have to give priority to private foster children. Fourth, the interviews with local authority welfare professionals in this book show that private fostering only receives adequate attention when a social worker concentrates on it. Fifth, the scope of the job is wider than most SSDs and SWDs seem to imagine. Consider the following:

- Working pro-actively to provide information about private fostering to both people likely to foster and welfare staff likely to come across potential and actual placements in order to make the notification system effective.
- Seeking out language schools, charities which bring refugees to Britain and asylum seekers to see if they make private fostering placements.
- Assessing potential and actual private foster carers.
- If necessary taking the sometimes complex legal steps to prohibit unsuitable carers and to remove children from dangerous situations.
- Providing help, guidance, training, support and sometimes material assistance to private foster carers.
- Visiting, listening to, counselling and ensuring the well-being of private foster children. This may well involve co-operating with education and health services.

- Making and maintaining contact with the natural parents before and during placements and perhaps helping them to arrange a smooth transition of their child back to their care.
- Providing evidence for courts which are dealing with foster carers' applications for residence orders over private foster children.
- Forming links with BAAF, and other agencies in order to increase knowledge about and interest in private fostering.

This list is probably not complete. But it is sufficient to show that responsibility for private fostering has to be in the hands of a specialist who makes it their major task. Indeed, in local authorities with larger numbers of private foster children, a team of specialists will be required. Preferably, at least one member should be West African.

Both the second and third approaches are linked with the private fostering social workers reporting to the adoption and fostering panel. Any decisions about new private fostering placements are thus made not by a lone manager but by a team of experienced people. I believe the panels should also contain a health visitor. As Beverley Clarke made clear in her interview, health visitors have often visited many homes where private foster children aged under five are living. They thus know much not just about care by natural parents but also that by foster parents.

Face to Face Practice

The establishment of a notification system that works and the readiness to appoint specialist private fostering social workers is just the framework of practice. Within this, the most important aspect of the work is the kind of relationships these workers form with natural parents, private foster carers and private foster children, that is with face to face practice. In this section, drawing heavily upon the experience of the professionals I interviewed and upon the official Guidance and Regulations which followed the 1989 Act, I will attempt to describe what I regard as good private fostering practice.

If contact is made with natural parents before they part with their children, then *preventative work* becomes possible. Within SSDs and SWDs, family support by which social workers attempt to improve the quality of children's lives so that they can remain within their own families rather than entering public care, has, according to Jane Tunstill, declined in recent decades (Tunstill, 1999, p126). Prevention in regard to private foster children has been almost non-existent. In her interview, Beverley Clarke commented, 'Most people who use private fostering do so in response to child care and poverty needs. If we were working in a preventive way and addressed these needs, we could avoid some of the subsequent tragedies'.

Yet another reason for concentrating private fostering in the hands of specialists is that they are more likely to have the time and motivation to undertake preventative work with parents. The aim should not be to dissuade them at all costs from placing their children with private foster carers. Rather it is to explore with them whether this is really what they want and whether it suits the needs of their children. Iris Amoah, in her interview, pointed out that some West Africans were having to work long and unsocial hours just to earn enough to survive and so could not cope with their children at home. Private fostering social workers could examine with them whether they are receiving their full wage entitlements and what difference it would make if their children stayed at home and they claimed, if eligible, the Working Families Tax Credit. They could also discuss whether some form of day care was suitable and, if so, what was available to them. In the cases of parents wanting to put their teenage children elsewhere because they could not cope with them, the private fostering specialists could offer to mediate between parents and children and, perhaps, introduce the children to youth clubs or neighbourhood projects which would give them constructive leisure and relieve some of the pressure on the parents. If, despite these efforts, the parents were pressing ahead with private fostering and had private foster carers in mind, the social worker would be likely to know whether the latter were disqualified persons or unsuitable in other ways.

Once a notification is made to the local authority, whether by the private foster carers or the parents, or as soon as they learn that a child is in a private foster home, then the private fostering social worker must *assess the suitability of the carers and their premises.* Immediately they must undertake police checks to see if the carers or other members of their household are disqualified persons under Section 68 of the Children Act (1989) and like legislation for Scotland. This Section refers, for instance, to people whose rights over their own children have been removed or who have committed offences against children. If they are disqualified, then official letters would be sent telling them they could not receive the children. If they already have the children, the letter would instruct them to return the children to the parents and, if they failed to comply, legal action would be taken to remove the children. The private fostering specialist should also quickly ascertain whether the proposed or actual carers had a history of violence or other dangerous behaviour towards children and should take up references from people who can comment objectively on their parenting capacities.

The assessment of private foster carers requires both skills and sensitivity. Skills because the private fostering social workers will be predicting how the carers are likely to treat children (or how they are treating them if they are already there) and sensitivity in that the initial contacts with the carers may determine how they co-operate with the SSDs and SWDs in the future.

In compiling their report on the private foster carers, the specialist workers should give attention to the following factors amongst others:

- Their parenting capacities in regard to the particular age of the private foster children. Coping with babies is different from coping with teenagers.

- Their attitude towards discipline with the understanding that harsh and corporal punishment is not acceptable.
- Their insights into the effect that separation can have on the behaviour of children.
- Their readiness and ability to help black children to understand and have access to their own backgrounds, culture, religion, diet and language.
- The ability to attend to children's health needs, including a willingness to take them to regular health checks and to provide them with a nutritious diet.
- The understanding that children require appropriate play and leisure opportunities.
- Where applicable, their readiness to encourage children in their schooling.
- Their appreciation that foster children usually benefit from regular and frequent contact with their natural parents and their siblings.

The social workers should also explain why the potential (or actual) children are being placed by their parents and what have been the children's previous experiences including other separations. Where the children are already there, observations can be made about their behaviour and contentment. Where applicable social workers should also comment upon other members of the household and, in particular, the likely or actual effects of foster children on the private foster carers' own children.

In addition, the private fostering social workers should report on the suitability of the carers' premises. Children should have their own beds and, if aged over two, preferably should not share with older people. They should not be put in conditions of overcrowding and, as a general rule, the Guidance and Regulations, recommend that no private foster home should have more than three foster children. The premises should contain adequate play space both indoors and out. Attention should be given to the safety of the accommodation such as the standard of electrical fittings and the provision of stair gates for small children.

When complete, the social workers assessments go to their senior managers or preferably to the adoption and fostering panels. The Guidance and Regulations make clear that in assessing the suitability of the carers, the focus must be 'linked to the duty of the local authority to satisfy itself that the welfare of the child is being satisfactorily safeguarded and promoted while privately fostered' (Department of Health, 1991, para. 1.5.1). Their decision is no easy one for, as Heather Clacy explained in her interview, there are 'instances where the foster carers are not ideal, we would not accept them as local authority carers, but we allow it on the basis that the parents have made the choice but they also have to be assessed as suitable to privately foster'. The panel may decide that the private foster carers or their premises are not suitable then, under Section 69 of the Children Act (1989), they can prohibit them from fostering. The carers have a right to appeal against this decision. If foster children are already in the home, they have to be returned to the parents and, if this does not occur legal proceedings can follow, as described in Part V of the Children Act (1989), with the likelihood that the children are removed to the care of the local authorities.

Interestingly, Brendan McGrath reported that his department had never had to resort to court proceedings because he usually persuaded the natural parents to collect their children. He added, 'We have never even imposed a requirement on private foster carers. I talk to them and they will usually accept my suggestions'. In short, action is not just about following the steps itemised by legislation and regulations. It is also about how private fostering social workers use their skills in relationships to achieve what is best for the children in ways which encourage parents and foster carers to co-operate.

The panel may ask the private foster carers to make an improvement to the premises—such as fitting smoke alarms—before they make a final decision. If all is well, they will indicate that the private fostering arrangements are acceptable or satisfactory and the decision is conveyed to them. This does not mean that they have become 'approved foster carers'. A few local authorities, through the same mechanisms, also decide whether the private foster children are to be deemed as 'in need'. One of the main provisions of the Children Act (1989) was to place a duty on local authorities:

- To safeguard and promote the welfare of children within their area who are in need.
- In so far as is consistent with that duty, to promote the upbringing of such children by their families, by providing a range and level of services appropriate to those children's needs. (Section 17).

It added that children were to be taken as being in need if they were unlikely to achieve or maintain a reasonable standard of health or development, without the provision of services, if their health or development was likely to be significantly impaired without such services, and if they were disabled. The corresponding legislation in Scotland appeared in Section 22 of the Children (Scotland) Act (1995). The Guidance and Regulations made it clear that private foster children or children about to be privately fostered could be deemed as 'in need' if they fell within the criteria and added, 'The child's needs which are to be considered also include physical, emotional and educational needs according to his age, gender, race, religion, culture, and language' (Department of Health, 1991, para. 1.3.8).

Not all private foster children can or should be deemed by local authorities to be 'in need' Most young language students visiting Britain for over 28 days come within the private fostering regulations but, if safe provision is made for them, there is no point in classifying them as 'in need'. Further, consideration has to be given to the views of natural parents and private foster carers who might regard such classification as drawing them further into the statutory net, whereas they had chosen private fostering because they wanted a private arrangement. But the welfare of the child must come first and the private fostering social workers in their reports and the adoption and fostering unit (or other body which deals with it) have to consider whether the children's conditions and needs do fall within the specifications of the Act. One advantage of deeming private foster children as being 'in need' is that it legitimates using resources to help them from a local authority's 'in need' budget which is invariably larger than its private fostering one: if it exists at all. Money could be used both to enable children to have their needs met by staying with their natural parents and for the provision of services to support them while with the private foster parents. One instance that came from one of the professionals I met was of 'in need' money being used to pay £50 a week to private foster carers for a teenager whose parents had stopped paying them. These contributions probably meant that the local authority did not have to accommodate the teenager.

Once the private fostering arrangements have been approved, the private fostering social worker should settle into a routine of regularly *visiting the private foster homes*. The Guidance and Regulations stipulate that a visit has to be made within one week of the placement starting and then at intervals of not more than six weeks for the first year. In subsequent years, the intervals are not more than three months. These are the minimum visiting rates. If appropriate, social workers should call much more often. The aim of the visits relates back to the duty of local authorities to satisfy themselves that the welfare of the children 'is being properly safeguarded and promoted and to secure that such advice is given to those caring for them as appears to the authority to be needed' (Children Act (1989), Section 67).

The social workers should carry out two main roles towards the private foster parents. First, the inspectoral role. They must ensure that the children's health and emotional needs are being met. Where applicable, they would focus on whether the carers are ensuring that the children have knowledge about their cultural and racial backgrounds and contact with people from the same ethnic grouping. They should ask about the amount of contact between the children and their parents. They should discuss the children's educational progress and, where appropriate, visit schools and other agencies which have dealings with them.

Heather Clacy, from her wide experience of visiting private fosterings, said, 'The private foster carers often regard me with some suspicion. They see us as the authorities who remove children'. In order to lessen this suspicion, it is essential that, in the second place, the private fostering social workers have a supportive role. They could advise foster parents about any difficulties they are having with the children. Amongst the foster carers who were interviewed, it was those with demanding teenagers who felt they received insufficient guidance from social workers. Where necessary, they should discuss how the carers help the children when they face racial abuse from others or questions about why they do not live with their own parents. Often it is practical aid which carers appreciate and which becomes the springboard for closer relationships with the social workers. Social workers could draw upon resources to help pay the fees for young foster children to attend play groups, to provide some toys, to pay for the children to go on school trips, to tide them over periods when natural parents do not pay their fees. There are examples of private foster carers being paid to go on training courses, sometimes attending those arranged for local authority foster carers. Angus Geddes developed groups for white private foster carers with black children. They not only enabled the carers to learn more about how to help their children, the groups also became a forum of mutual support for the carers. Thereafter, Angus had close and positive individual relationships with the members. Lastly, the social workers should seek to clarify with the carers just what are the plans for the children and when they are to return home. The carers might ask for information about how they could obtain permanent care of the children. Social workers have a responsibility to explain about residence orders and adoption but should do so in the framework of what is best for the children and with consideration for the feelings and wishes of the natural parents.

The social workers are obliged to write reports on their visits and if the care of the children is not satisfactory then the local authority can still take action against carers in the ways described previously.

While visiting the private foster homes, the social workers are expected always to see the private foster children. They should seek the views of the children and the Guidance and Regulations say that, where of age, the children should be seen alone. Relating with and communicating with children separated from their own parents is one of the child care skills essential for this work. Some of the professionals interviewed for this study explained how they would sometimes take children to a cafe or to a leisure activity so that, in a more relaxed atmosphere, they could explain just why they were visiting. The social workers should display a genuine interest in whether the child is happy in the foster home, how they are progressing at school, and what is the nature of their contact with their own family. In some cases, and foster carers and natural parents should be kept informed, the social workers should be prepared to talk with children about their puzzlement, their sorrow, their anger about why they are not with their parents and also about their fears about having to be returned to them. Some disturbed children may require referrals to psychological services. The overall aim should be that a trusting relationship is formed so that, at any time, the children would feel free to contact their social worker. If this is achieved, then, at least, the situation will be avoided where abused or neglected private foster children feel there is no one to whom they can complain.

The Guidance and Regulations state, 'There is a basic principle throughout the Act that parents retain their responsibilities and shall remain as closely involved as is consistent with their child's welfare' (Department of Health, 1991, para 1.4.5.). The main Act, and corresponding legislation in Scotland, do not place a duty upon local authorities to pursue regular *meetings with the natural parents* but my view is that this is an essential part of good practice. Where the parents live hundreds of miles away, these may be time consuming and expensive. Some parents may live abroad but contact can still be sought through letters, phone and now e-mail. Meetings with parents are vital for these reasons:

- To enable parents (when they are seen before placements are made), to avoid unsuitable private foster carers. In addition, social workers can encourage the parents to introduce their children gradually to a new setting.
- To remind them that they are still responsible for the safety and well-being of their children.
- To keep the parents informed about how their children are progressing—or not—in the private foster homes.
- To continue to gather information about the children from the parents which may be useful to the private foster carers.
- To impress upon the parents the importance of visiting their children regularly. As stated in the last chapter, there may be cases where visits from dangerous or destructive parents are not wanted. Generally, however, contact with parents assures children that they are still loved by them and helps them know who they are and why they are in a foster home. Visits from black parents are particularly valuable to children with white carers where they may be struggling with understanding their own identity. From the interviews with the former foster children like Roland Webb, Mary Tapper and Margaret McMinn, it is clear that absence of contact caused them much distress and pain. For children who are deemed 'in need' and whose parents live miles away, it would be legitimate to provide the parents with some financial aid, if necessary, in order to facilitate visits.
- To prevent the parents and foster carers growing apart. There is no doubt that some private foster carers interpret a lack of visits as a sign that the parents do not want the children so that they then take legal steps to look after them permanently. But this may not have been the intention of the natural parents and the outcome can be long and painful litigation.
- To encourage the parents to plan the children's future and to keep the foster carers informed of it. If the private fostering social worker has formed a trusting relationship with the parents, they will welcome their advice in easing the children's eventual transition from the foster carers back to them again.
- To undertake after-care in conjunction with the parents. The experience of Yvonne Martins and the cases cited by Drs Taylor and Cook, in their interviews, reveal that private foster children can be unhappy and exhibit

disturbed behaviour when they do return home. This is most likely to happen when they have not been in regular contact with their parents. If they have been classified as 'in need' by the local authority, then social workers certainly can continue to help them. There is some confusion as to whether social workers can offer after-care services to private foster children after the age of 16. The Guidance and Regulations stipulate that former disabled private foster children can be helped until they are 21 (Department of Health, 1991, para. 1.8.19). But what of others? Private fostering social workers, and the legal departments which advise them, differ as to the interpretation of the legislation. The Department of Health should clarify the issue. But whatever the interpretation of the legislation, private fostering social workers could undertake after-care on a voluntary basis if the participants agree. The crux of the matter is whether, over the years, the social workers have built up the kind of relationships with the children which moves them to want to maintain contact. Successful involvement is more than about applying the law. It is about skilled social work.

The Reform of Private Fostering

This study has shown that many private foster children and private foster carers are not being satisfactorily safeguarded and served by local authorities. This chapter has suggested how the situation could be improved. The government in conjunction with local authorities could organise a more effective awareness campaign so that far more intended and actual placements are notified to SSDs and SWDs. Local authorities could install a framework which would include a private fostering policy statement and the appointment of private fostering social workers to report to their adoption and fostering panels. They could promote good practice in which these social workers undertook preventative work, assessments of the suitability of private fostering carers, and close relationships with private foster children, the carers and natural parents in order to ensure the best possible care for the children. All these improvements could occur within existing legislation and a few SSDs are already setting an example of what can be done. But most departments appear to be held back by a lack of resources and a lack of commitment to private fostering.

Three other improvements are necessary which will require changes in legislation and government policy.

1. Registration of private foster carers
As far back as the late 1950s, child care officers were calling for a system of registering private foster carers. In 1997, the Utting Report recommended, 'that private foster carers should be required to seek approval and registration from a local authority before taking on any children . . . To do so without registration should be a criminal offence. It should also be an offence for parents to place a

child with unregistered foster carers.' (Department of Health and the Welsh Office, 1997, para. 3.80.)

Registration is backed by BAAF and by the welfare professionals interviewed in this book as the single most important step to help private fostering for these reasons:

- It would mean that more natural parents would approach SSDs and SWDs in order to get the names of registered carers. Not only would social workers be able to steer them away from unsuitable carers, the social workers would be able to work with the parents in order to prepare the children for their new home.
- The overall standard of private foster carers would be improved. The unsuitable ones would not be registered and would be breaking the law if they did foster. Potential foster carers would learn that standards of parenting and premises were required. Those registered would be offered some resources and training.
- Most important, the safeguarding of private foster children would be increased because they should be placed only with carers who are known to and approved by the local authority. Moreover, where children were placed with illegal carers, the local authority could take action against them simply on the grounds that they were not on the register without having to go through the present sometimes long-drawn-out process of proving them unsuitable before a court.

Minders who take in children on a daily basis are now required to be registered. In his interview, Brendan McGrath drew a comparison, 'In child minding, once the concept of registration came in, standards improved. The same would happen if private foster carers had to be registered. Registration would offer a status and approval, which our present system of just accepting the private foster carers does not.' It might well be that registered carers would have a pride in their position and would report any unregistered ones.

The Utting proposal for registration of private foster carers was just one of many proposals in a report which covered a wide range of children. In 1998, the government issued *The Government's Response to the Children's Safeguards Review*. It accepted many of Utting's recommendations to protect children living away from home but with one notable exception: the registration of private foster carers. The government stated, 'The government will not seek legislation to require local authorities to register private foster parents. It does not consider that a new system of regulation is necessary as there is already a wide range of offences associated with private fostering and the Government does not believe it would be right to extend them further' (Department of Health, 1998, para 3.4). If carers who look after children during the day have to be registered then it seems odd that those who look after them for months or years do not. What explains the government's refusal to act? Some commentators believe that institutional racism plays a part and that the government is not interested because many private foster children are black. Perhaps so, although it must be added that many daily minded children are also black. Another view is that the government is reluctant to intervene in what is essentially a private arrangement. But, again, child minding is also a private arrangement. Indeed, the government is to make regulations governing agencies which supply nannies with particular reference to the latters' qualifications and histories. In short, it is even prepared to interfere in the private arrangements of middle class parents who can afford nannies. Whatever the merits of these arguments, the overwhelming case for a register of private foster carers is that it would make some private foster children less liable to abuse and it would raise the standards of the care given to them.

The case for registration is still being made. An Adoption Bill will shortly come before parliament and BAAF is campaigning for an amendment which will bring a register for private foster carers into being. It is possible, therefore, that it could soon be on the statute books. Registration would be essential but it would not be sufficient. Registration will not improve the quality and extent of social work with natural parents and it will not provide hard-pressed local authorities with resources for private fostering work.

2. A duty towards natural parents

Hopefully this study has shown that the involvement of natural parents is essential to the well-being of private foster children. They choose the private foster carers for their children. If they visit regularly then their contact can both lessen any problems with the carers and give the children a sense of their own identity. Their continuing closeness to the children can smooth their eventual transition back to them. Yet it appears that numbers of parents do not fequently see their children. Local authorities do not have a duty to meet regularly with the natural parents. My proposal is that existing legislation be amended to stipulate that, unless contrary to the interests of the children, local authorities, if at all possible, should meet with the natural parents at least every two months in the first year of a placement and at least every three months thereafter.

3. The provision of resources

One explanation why local authorities have neglected their responsibilities towards private fosterings is that they have lacked the money. Few, if any, have a private fostering budget. Some of the welfare professionals I met, said that they pushed to have private foster children deemed as 'in need' as this made them eligible for Section 17 money, that is the budget for 'in need' children according to the Children Act (1989). They added that area teams might then resent private foster children having access to their area's 'in need' allocation.

If private fostering is ever to be a priority then it must have sufficient resources. I have already indicated that private fostering should be included in the government's Quality Protects programme with a budget to match. Further, my proposal is that central government should 'ring fence' a private foster grant to local authorities, that is, it could be spent only on private fosterings. How much money? I suggest that the Department of Health should pay half the salary of just one private fostering specialist plus £2,000 a year for every notified private foster child. For England and Wales, I calculate that staff costs would be about £2.7 million and, given around 9,500 private foster children, £19 million for the children. The total annual amount would be about £22 million which is a mere fraction of the expenditure of the Department of Health. A local authority with 100 private foster children would receive £200,000 from the per head grant. They could use this towards the other half of the private fostering specialist, for additional staff, and for money to support the private foster children, carers and natural parents. Indeed, SSDs and SWDs would have an incentive to detect as many private foster children as possible as this would increase their financial allocation.

But can improvements be promoted? Private fostering receives less attention now than in the 1950s and 1960s when the Association of Child Care Officers and the Association of Children's Officers regularly had private fostering on their agendas. Today BAAF and the Private Fostering Special Interest Group of the Health Visitors Association are concerned but have limited resources. It is time for the Association of Directors of Social Services and the British Association of Social Workers to combine with these agencies, with other interested bodies and with former private foster children and present private foster carers and natural parents to form a private fostering lobby.

At present, social work training courses include little about private fostering. The lobby could encourage them to cover it fully. This would mean that some new social workers would be aware of and knowledgeable about private fostering. After work experience in other forms of child care, they should then be equipped with the specialist skills to be private fostering social workers.

Just as important, the lobby should campaign for the changes proposed in this chapter, that is, the registration of private foster carers, the duty to visit regularly the natural parents, and the allocation of central funds for local authority private fostering social work. These reforms are vital both for the safeguarding and the well-being of private foster children and also for supporting those private foster carers who can offer satisfactory care to the children. Hopefully, government will respond to the lobby. If not, it probably will not act until it is pushed into action by a public inquiry into the sexual abuse, neglect or death of a private foster child. And this will be too late for at least one child.

Bibliography

Abrams, L. (1998) *The Orphan Country*. John Donald Publishers.

African Family Advisory Service (1997) *Private Fostering. Development and Practice in Three English Local Authorities*. Save the Children.

Association of Directors of Social Services (2001) *Local Authorities and Private Fostering. ADSS Survey*. Bedfordshire County Council.

Avon Social Services Department (1987). Letter to author.

Ayotte, W. (2000) *Separated Children Coming to Europe*. Save the Children.

Batty, D. (Ed.) (1995) *Other People's Children. A Guide for Private Foster Carers*. British Agencies for Adoption and Fostering.

Batty, D. with Wrighton, P. (1996). *Foster Care. A Guide for Birth Parents Considering Private Fostering*. British Agencies for Adoption and Fostering.

Berridge, D. (1997) *A Research Review*. The Stationery Office.

British Agencies for Adoption and Fostering (1997) *BAAF Warns of Children at Risk in Private Fostering*. Press release.

Bullard, E. and Malos, E. with Parker, R. (1990) *A Report to the Department of Health on the Implementation of Part Two of the Children Act 1975 in England and Wales From December 1985 to December 1988*. University of Bristol.

Collier, F. (1998) Invisible Placements Can't be Policed. *Community Care*. 5 Nov.

Commonwealth Students' Children's Society (1975) *The African Child in Great Britain*.

Community Relations Commission (1975) *Fostering Black Children*.

Cook, S. (1983) Fostering trouble. *The Guardian*. 9 Nov.

Davies, C. (1998) *Sunday with Hayes*. Interview on Five Live. 22 Nov.

Department of Health (1991) *The Children Act 1989. Guidance and Regulations. Volume 8. Private Fostering and Miscellaneous*. The Stationery Office.

Department of Health (1998) *The Government's Response to the Children's Safeguards Review*. The Stationery Office.

Department of Health (2000a) *Annual Report of the Chief Inspector of the Social Services Inspectorate 1999–2000. Modern Social Services. A Commitment to People*. HMSO.

Department of Health (2000b) *Crackdown on Private Fostering*. Press release.

Department of Health (2001) *Private fostering. A Cause for Concern*. Pamphlet.

Department of Health and the Welsh Office (1997) *People Like Us. The Report of the Review of the Safeguards for Children Living Away from Home*. The Stationery Office. (Utting Report.)

Diogenes (1973) Law Report. *New Society*, 8 March.

Geddes, A. (1990) *Report on West African Fostering in Swindon Between 1988–1990.* Wiltshire County Council.

Gibbs, G. (1999) Children on Foreign Trips at Risk of Abuse. *The Guardian.* 28 Jul.

Gilroy, P. (2001) Away From Home, Alone. *Community Care.* 2 Aug.

Glasgow Social Work Sub Committee (1998) *Prioritisation of Work Within Area Teams.* Glasgow Social Work Department.

Goldstein, J., Freud, A. and Solnit, A. (1973) *Beyond the Best Interests of the Child.* The Free Press.

The Guardian, Reports on Law Cases. 5 Dec 1972 and 15 Feb 1973.

Heywood, J. (1959) *Children in Care.* Routledge and Kegan Paul.

Holman, B. (1973) *Trading in Children. A study of Private Fostering.* Routledge and Kegan Paul.

Holman, B. (1996) *The Corporate Parent. Manchester Children's Department 1948–1971.* National Institute for Social Work.

Home Office (1961) *Eighth Report of the Work of the Children's Department.* HMSO.

Home Office (1967) *Report on the Work of the Children's Departments 1964–1966.* HMSO.

Home Office, Ministry of Health and Ministry of Education (1946) *Report of the Care of Children Committee.* (Curtis Report). HMSO.

Hopkirk, M. (1949) *Nobody Wanted Sam.* John Murray.

House of Commons (1984) *Second Report from the Social Services Committee 1983–84, Children in Care.* (Short Report). HMSO.

Ince, L. (1998) *Making it Alone.* British Agencies for Adoption and Fostering.

Lambeth Social Services Department (1986) Letter to the author. Dec.

Middleton, N. (1971) *When Family Failed.* Gollancz.

National Institute for Social Work (1982) *Social Workers: Their Role and Tasks.* (Barclay Report). Bedford Square Press.

Packman, J. (1975) *The Child's Generation.* Blackwell and Robertson.

Philpot, T. (2001) *A Very Private Practice. An Investigation into Private Fostering.* British Agencies for Adoption and Fostering.

Race Equality Unit (1993) *Black Children and Private Fostering.* National Institute for Social Work.

Rickford, F. (1992) Private Means. *Community Care.* 18 Jun.

Rickford, F. (1995) Hidden from view. *Health Visitor*, no. 12, December.

Rickford, F. (1998) Mixed Emotions. *The Guardian.* 22 Apr.

Ruddock, K. (1949) *Annual Report of the Children's Officer 1948–49.* County of Leicester Children's Committee.

Ruddock, K. (1951) *Annual Report of the Children's Officer 1950–51.* County of Leicester Children's Committee.

Ruddock, K. (1963) *Report of the Children's Officer 1961–63.* County of Leicester Children's Committee.

Ruddock, K. (1969) *Report of the Children's Officer 1967–69.* County of Leicester Children's Committee.

Scottish Education Department and Social Work Services Group (1975) *Report of the Committee of Inquiry into the Consideration Given and Steps Taken Towards Securing the Welfare of Richard Clark by Perth Town Council and Other Bodies or Persons Concerned.* HMSO.

Scottish Home Department (1946) *Report of the Committee on Homeless Children.* (Clyde Report). HMSO.

Scottish Office (1997) *Children's Safeguards Review.* (Kent Report).The Stationery Office.

Scottish Office (1998) *The Scottish Office Response to the Children's Safeguards Review.* The Stationery Office.

Social Services Inspectorate (1994) *Signposts. Findings from a National Inspection of Private Fostering.* Department of Health.

Social Services Inspectorate (1997) Letter from Chief Inspector of the Social Services Inspectorate to author. Nov.

Social Services Inspectorate (2000) Letter from the Chief Inspector to Directors of Social Services.

Stein, M. (2000) *Missing Out.* Aberlour Trust.

Stone, K. (1990) A private practice. *Community Care.* 21 Jun.

Traynor, J. (2001) Losing Touch. *The Guardian.* 25 Jul.

Tunstill, J. (Ed.) (1999) *Children and the State. Whose problem?* Cassell.

Woollard, C. and Clarke, B. (1999) Private Fostering, in Wheal, A. (Ed.) *Companion to Foster Care.* Russell House Publishing.